Yoshida's
FINE SAUCES

YOSHIDA CLASSICS

recipe collection

A collection from customers, family & friends.

Y

"...I hope you enjoy my sauce as much as I enjoy bringing it to you."

Junki Yoshida

Published by YOSHIDA® FOOD PRODUCTS CO.

Designed and Art Directed by
Rebecca J. Reinke
Studio Photography by
Michael Shay, Steve Cherry
Polara Studio
Food Styling by Carol Cooper Ladd, Lucy Radys

Printed in the U.S.A. by Graphic Arts Center, Portland, OR

Any inquiries should be directed to the
YOSHIDA® FOOD PRODUCTS CO.
8440 NE Alderwood Rd. Suite A
Portland, OR 97220 (800) 653–1114

Appetizers

SPICY PRAWN COCKTAIL
2

BACON & OLIVE STUFFED MUSHROOMS
2

MARINATED SUMMER TOMATOES
4

EGGROLLS
4

LUAU MEATBALLS
5

PANACHE ROLL-UPS
5

PARTY POTATOES
8

MIXED NUTS & GOURMET SAUCE
8

INDONESIAN COCONUT PRAWNS
10

RIB & CHICKEN APPETIZER PLATTER
10

BUFFALO WINGS
12

SWEET & SOUR LIL' SMOKIES
12

Spicy Prawn Cocktail

Spicy Prawn Cocktail

serves six to eight

2 cups *Yoshida's® Classic Red Sweet & Sour Sauce*
1 teaspoon cayenne pepper sauce, as desired *(Tobasco)*
1 zucchini, julienne sliced
1 carrot, julienne sliced
1 cucumber, sliced razor thin
1 pound chilled cooked prawns, *(16–20 per pound)* peeled and deveined
cilantro and chives *(optional garnish)*

❧ Mix *Yoshida's®* with pepper sauce in a small bowl.

❧ In another small bowl, toss the zucchini and carrots with 1/4 cup of the sauce.

❧ To arrange plate for serving: lay cucumbers in a scallop pattern over the bottom of the plate. Swirl some of the remaining sauce over cucumbers. Place a small, high mound of vegetables in center of the plate and set the prawns around the edges. Swirl some sauce over the prawns. Garnish the mound with a sprig of cilantro and chive if desired.

❧ Serve remaining sauce on the side for dipping.

Bacon & Olive Stuffed Mushrooms

makes thirty

4 slices bacon, cooked and crumbled
1/4 cup drained and chopped olives
1/2 cup grated Parmesan cheese
3 tablespoons *Yoshida's® Original Gourmet Sauce*
1 small onion, grated
30 large mushrooms, stems removed

❧ Make the filling by mixing bacon, olives, cheese, sauce and onion in a small bowl. Set aside.

❧ Preheat oven to 350° F.

❧ Gently clean the mushrooms with a damp paper towel. Arrange, cavity side up, in a baking dish. Divide the filling evenly among the mushroom caps.

❧ Set baking dish in upper third of the oven and bake for 15 minutes. Change the oven setting to broil. Broil for 5 minutes or until the filling is browned. Serve hot.

Appetizers

Marinated Summer Tomatoes

Marinated Summer Tomatoes

serves four

4 medium tomatoes, cut in 1/4" slices
(or a colorful variety of assorted tomatoes)
1/8 teaspoon salt
3 tablespoons *Yoshida's® Yakiniku Sauce*
2 tablespoons olive oil
2 tablespoons red wine vinegar or rice wine vinegar
2 cloves fresh garlic, finely chopped
fresh basil for garnish

❧ Wash and slice tomatoes. Arrange them on a glass or ceramic plate. Mix remaining ingredients for dressing and drizzle over tomatoes.

❧ Cover and let marinate at room temperature for 1–3 hours. Garnish plate with the basil. Serve.

Eggrolls

makes twelve to thirteen

1 cup *Yoshida's® Hawaiian Sweet & Sour Sauce*
2 cups finely diced cooked pork
1 medium carrot, julienne sliced
1 stalk celery, julienne sliced
1 cup bean sprouts
1 package of eggroll wrappers
1 cup vegetable oil

❧ In a medium–sized bowl, mix *Yoshida's®* with pork, carrot, celery and sprouts. Lay each wrapper down, one at a time and spoon 2 tablespoons (or more depending on size of wrappers) of filling in the lower center of wrapper with wrapper facing you in a diamond shape. Fold the short sides in and roll up. Use a little water on the top point to help seal roll. Set aside with seam sides down while the oil heats.

❧ Heat oil in a large skillet over medium–high and fry eggrolls in batches until golden brown, about 5 minutes. Drain on paper towels. Serve with dipping sauces.

Appetizers

Luau Meatballs

party appetizer

1 3 pound bag beef meatballs
1 small can pineapple chunks, drained
4 cups *Yoshida's®Hawaiian Sweet & Sour Sauce*

❧ Brown meatballs in batches over medium–high heat in a large skillet for 10–15 minutes.

❧ Remove cooked meatballs to a serving dish and sprinkle pineapple chunks around the meatballs.

❧ Heat the *Yoshida's®* in a small saucepan. When hot, pour over the meatballs to coat well.

❧ Serve meatballs with toothpicks.

Panache Roll-Ups

serves eight

1/4 cup nonfat sour cream
1/3 cup picante sauce
1 tablespoon garlic powder
1/3 cup *Yoshida's® Spicy Wing & Rib Sauce*
8 warmed tortillas
16 ounces reduced fat cream cheese
1 1/2 pounds turkey breast, thinly sliced
1 cup sliced olives

❧ Make the filling by combining sour cream, picante sauce, garlic powder and *Yoshida's®*. To assemble roll–ups, spread each tortilla with 4 tablespoons of the cream cheese. Portion turkey breast on next, covering the cream cheese. Spoon 2 tablespoons of the filling over the turkey and sprinkle 2 tablespoons olives over the filling. Roll up the tortilla as tightly as possible. Holding it seam side down, cut off the ends. Cut each roll–up into 2 or 3 pieces.

❧ Arrange the roll–ups on a platter and garnish with the green onions.

Appetizers

Panache Roll–Ups

Party Potatoes

Party Potatoes

makes twenty

20 baby red potatoes
1/4 teaspoon ground pepper
1/3 cup melted butter
1/2 cup *Yoshida's® Hawaiian Sweet & Sour Sauce*
8 ounces cream cheese
1/3 cup sour cream
1/2 teaspoon salt
paprika *(garnish)*
chives *(garnish)*

❧ Boil the potatoes until just tender and set aside to cool. When cool enough to handle, slice off the top and bottom of each potato (so they sit flat) and carefully scoop out most of the pulp, leaving a layer 1/8" thick around the sides. Be careful not to tear through the skin. (You may use an iced tea spoon or small baby spoon for scooping.) Put all of the cooked potato pulp into a medium–sized bowl.

❧ Preheat the oven to 375° F.

❧ Add the remaining ingredients, except paprika and chives, to the bowl with the potato pulp and mix well. Using a pastry bag (or a plastic baggy with a corner cut off), pipe the filling back into each potato. As you fill each potato, pipe a decorative swirl on each top. Place the filled potatoes on a baking sheet. Sprinkle with paprika and bake in the top 1/3 of the oven for 20 minutes or until heated through and golden. To serve you may wish to garnish the plate with chives.

Mixed Nuts & Gourmet Sauce

makes two pounds

2 pounds unsalted almonds and pecans
1 cup *Yoshida's® Original Gourmet Sauce*

❧ Place mixed nuts in a bowl and cover with sauce. Cover bowl and let nuts soak for 1 hour, stirring occasionally to ensure even coating. Strain nuts and set aside.

❧ Spray or grease an 8"x10" glass baking dish and spread 1 cup of the soaked nuts in the bottom of the pan. Cook them in the microwave on high for 4 to 5 minutes, stirring at two minute intervals. Allow to cool then spread on a tray. Repeat the process until all nuts are cooked. Serve.

Appetizers

Indonesian Coconut Prawns

Indonesian Coconut Prawns

serves four

1 pound prawns, *(16–20 per pound)*, peeled and deveined
1 cup *Yoshida's® Original Gourmet Sauce*
1/4 cup unsalted roasted peanuts
1 5 ounce can sliced water chestnuts, drained
1/4 cup chopped green onions
coconut, shredded
2 cups cooked white rice

❧ In a large skillet over medium heat, sautè prawns about 1 minute or until almost done. Remove prawns from the skillet and set aside.

❧ Drain excess liquid from the pan and add *Yoshida's®.* Reduce the sauce over medium–high heat until it starts to thicken into a glaze.

❧ Return the prawns to the pan along with the peanuts and water chestnuts. Return mixture to a simmer and remove from the heat.

❧ Assemble dish: On each plate, place a mound of rice in the center. Spoon peanuts and water chestnuts on and around rice. Place prawns around the base of the rice and sprinkle green onions and coconut over the entire dish. Serve immediately.

Rib & Chicken Appetizer Platter

party appetizer

1 1/2 cups *Yoshida's® Spicy Wing & Rib Sauce*
1 1/2 pounds chicken drumettes
2 pounds baby back ribs, cut in pieces
1/2 head iceburg lettuce, shredded fine

❧ Preheat oven to 400°F.

❧ In large bowl, toss 3/4 cup of sauce with drumettes and spread onto a baking sheet. In same bowl, add remaining sauce and toss with rib pieces. Spread pieces out on another baking sheet. Bake drumettes and ribs for about 35–45 minutes or until cooked through.

❧ Line a large serving platter with lettuce and arrange meat over greens. Serve while hot.

Appetizers

Buffalo Wings

Buffalo Wings

makes twenty-five

2–4 teaspoons crushed red chili pepper
1 clove fresh garlic, minced
1/2 teaspoon Chinese five spice powder
3/4 cup *Yoshida's® Original Gourmet Sauce*
25 chicken wingettes

❧ Preheat oven to 375°F. Place wings on a baking sheet.

❧ In a small bowl, stir together chili pepper, garlic, five spice and *Yoshida's.®* Pour sauce over wingettes and turn to coat.

❧ Bake wingettes on middle shelf of the oven for 45 minutes, or until cooked through and glazed.

Sweet & Sour Lil' Smokies

makes one pound

1 pound cocktail sausages
1 cup *Yoshida's® Hawaiian Sweet & Sour Sauce*

❧ Place sausages in a crockpot and turn temperature to high.

❧ Add *Yoshida's®* and stir well. Heat for 1 hour or until very hot. Serve immediately.

Appetizers

Marinades, Dips & Spreads

Oriental Vegetable Dip
13

Shrimp Stuffed Cabbage
13

Cream Cheese Spread
15

Chinese Style Marinade for Pork
15

Orange & Soy Marinade
16

Garlic & Mustard Marinade
16

Original Chicken Marinade
18

Hot & Spicy Dipping Sauce
18

Spicy Dipping Sauce
20

Gourmet Ginger Sauce
20

Oriental Vegetable Dip

makes three cups

1/2 cup softened cream cheese
1/2 cup mayonnaise
1/2 cup sour cream
1 tablespoon fresh lemon juice
3/4 cup *Yoshida's® Classic Red Sweet & Sour Sauce*
1/4 cup finely diced green bell peppers
1/4 cup finely diced green onions
1/4 cup finely chopped carrots
1/2 cup cooked, pressed spinach
(roll in paper towel or cheesecloth and squeeze to eliminate liquid)
pinch black pepper *(to taste)*
pinch garlic powder *(to taste)*
pinch salt *(to taste)*

❧ In a medium–sized mixing bowl, whisk the cream cheese, mayonnaise, sour cream and lemon juice together until smooth. Add *Yoshida's®* and blend. Fold in the vegetables and season to taste with pepper, garlic powder and salt.

❧ Chill.

Shrimp Stuffed Cabbage

1 medium size red cabbage
1 tablespoon minced onion
1 tablespoon lemon juice
8 ounces cream cheese, softened
2 tablespoons mayonnaise
1/4 cup *Yoshida's® Spicy Wing & Rib Sauce*
1 4 1/2 ounce can broken shrimp
2 tablespoons chopped dill pickle
1 tablespoon chopped parsely
paprika

❧ Remove two large cabbage leaves and arrange on plate to create a bowl shape.

❧ Mix together the onion, lemon juice, cream cheese, mayonnaise and *Yoshida's®.* Drain and coarsely chop the shrimp. Blend into cheese mixture with pickles and parsley. Transfer dip to cabbage "bowl" and gently pack in. Sprinkle with paprika. Keep chilled until ready to serve.

❧ Use as a dip or spread for toasted bread, crackers, or vegetables.

Dips

Shrimp Stuffed Cabbage

CREAM CHEESE SPREAD

makes four cups

3 cups softened cream cheese
3/4 cup *Yoshida's® Classic Red Sweet & Sour Sauce*
1/4 cup finely chopped green onion
1/4 cup finely chopped green pepper
1/4 cup drained and chopped ripe olives
salt and pepper *(to taste)*
Tobasco or other pepper sauce *(optional for spicy)*

❧ In a medium–sized bowl, blend the cream cheese with all remaining ingredients and transfer to a decorative bowl. Chill.

❧ Serve as a spread for bagels, bread, crackers or as a topping for canapes.

CHINESE STYLE MARINADE FOR PORK

1/2 cup Hoisen sauce
1/2 cup *Yoshida's® Original Gourmet Sauce*
1/3 cup *Yoshida's® Premium Steak Sauce*
2 tablespoons brown sugar
2 or 3 garlic cloves, minced
1 tablespoon sherry
1 tablespoon honey

❧ Mix all ingredients together. Cover both sides of meat and marinate at least 2 hours.

Shirley Vornali   Petaluma, CA

Marinades

15

ORANGE & SOY MARINADE

---

2 cups *Yoshida's® Original Gourmet Sauce*
1/2 cup brown sugar
1/2 cup soy sauce
1/2 cup orange soda
3 green onions, chopped
3 cloves fresh garlic, minced

❧ Combine all ingredients in a bowl and marinate your favorite meat such as beef, pork or chicken for 2–3 hours. This marinade is great for baking or grilling.

Liz Vogelgesang   Hereford, AR

GARLIC & MUSTARD MARINADE

1/2 cup *Yoshida's® Premium Steak Sauce*
1/2 cup *Yoshida's® Original Gourmet Sauce*
1/3 cup sherry
3 tablespoons Dijon mustard
1 teaspoon dried rosemary
4 or 5 cloves fresh garlic, crushed

❧ Mix all ingredients together. Marinate meat at least 1 hour or overnight. Great on ribs.

Shirley Vornali   Petaluma, CA

Marinades

Marinades and Sauces

Original Chicken Marinade

1 cup *Yoshida's® Original Gourmet Sauce*
1 tablespoon sesame seeds, plain or toasted
1/4 cup green onions *(scallions)*

❧ Combine *Yoshida's®* sesame seeds and green onions in a bowl. Marinate chicken for 3–4 hours or overnight.

Judy Fabilenia   Rafib, TX

Hot & Spicy Dipping Sauce

makes three fourths of a cup

1/2 cup *Yoshida's® Classic Red Sweet & Sour Sauce*
1 teaspoon crushed red chiles
3 tablespoons oriental hot mustard
4 tablespoons toasted sesame seeds

❧ In a small bowl, mix *Yoshida's®* with the chiles.

❧ Spoon the mustard into center of the *Yoshida's®* sauce and with a knife or toothpick draw swirls from mustard into the sauce for a decorative pattern.

❧ Dip eggrolls, wontons or potstickers into sauce and sesame seeds.

Marinades & Sauces

Spicy Dipping Sauce

19

SPICY DIPPING SAUCE

1/4 cup *Yoshida's® Original Gourmet Sauce*
1/4–1/2 teaspoon cayenne pepper

❧ Combine sauce with cayenne and warm in microwave about 30 seconds.

❧ Serve with potstickers and eggrolls.

Janet Skelton   Rancho Cordova, CA

Sauces

GOURMET GINGER SAUCE

makes one half cup

1/4 cup *Yoshida's® Original Gourmet Sauce*
1/4 cup fresh orange juice
6 slices fresh ginger
3 tablespoons Balsamic vinegar
1/2 teaspoon cornstarch
1 tablespoon water

❧ In a small saucepan stir together *Yoshida's,* orange juice, ginger and vinegar over medium–high heat. Bring the sauce to a boil. Turn heat down to low and simmer for 10 minutes or until the sauce reduces by 1/4.

❧ Mix cornstarch with water and pour into sauce. Stir until thickened.

❧ This sauce works well when served with roast, chicken, pork loin or sirloin strip steak.

Bob Pinne   Petaluma, CA

Breakfast & Brunch

Zucchini & Mushroom Frittata
22

Farmer's Breakfast Casserole
22

Sausage & Egg Breakfast Surprise
23

Breakfast Burritos
23

Creamy Cheddar & Potato Casserole
25

Pineapple Brunch Casserole
25

Mushroom, Spinach & Tomato Quiche
26

Zucchini & Mushroom Frittata

21

Zucchini & Mushroom Frittata

serves three to four

4 eggs
1/4 cup *Yoshida's® Premium Steak Sauce*
1/2 zucchini, sliced
1/2 cup sliced mushrooms
1/2 cup chopped green onions
3/4 cup grated Mozzarella cheese
6 ounces cooked linguini noodles, chilled

❧ In a medium–sized bowl, beat eggs until foaming. Mix in *Yoshida's®* and stir well. Fold in vegetables and pasta. Set aside.

❧ Heat a large non–stick ovenproof skillet over medium–low heat and pour in egg mixture.

❧ Sprinkle grated cheese over the eggs and continue to cook for a few minutes to set the bottom.

❧ Heat broiler and move oven rack to the middle position. When the eggs are set on the bottom, slide the pan under the broiler to finish cooking the frittata. Watch carefully to avoid browning the top.

❧ Slice while still warm and serve for breakfast, brunch or dinner.

Farmer's Breakfast Casserole

serves four to six

3 medium baking potatoes, peeled & cubed into bite size pieces
6–8 bacon slices, diced
1/4 cup minced onion
1 cup grated Swiss cheese
1/2 cup cottage cheese
5 eggs, beaten
1/4 cup *Yoshida's® Hawaiian Sweet & Sour Sauce*
1/2 teaspoon salt

❧ Cook potatoes until tender by boiling in water for 5 minutes or by microwaving on high for 8 minutes.

❧ In a heated skillet, cook bacon until browned and with a slotted spoon transfer to a paper towel to drain. Reserve the bacon drippings in skillet. Add cooked potatoes and the onions to the heated skillet and cook until golden brown, about 5 minutes. With a slotted spoon transfer the potatoes and onions to a bowl.

❧ Preheat oven to 350° F.

❧ Mix all remaining ingredients together in bowl with the potatoes and onions. Place mixture in a 9"x13" baking pan and bake for 30–40 minutes or until set in the center. Serve hot.

Breakfast

Breakfast

Sausage & Egg Breakfast Surprise

serves eight

1 1/2 pounds bulk sausage
8 bread slices, crust removed & cubed
4 eggs
2 1/4 cups milk
1/4 cup *Yoshida's® Original Gourmet Sauce*
2 teaspoons prepared mustard
1 teaspoon salt
1 can Cream of Mushroom soup
1/2–3/4 cup milk
2 cups shredded Cheddar cheese

🌿 The night before serving, fry the sausage and drain. Arrange the cubed bread in bottom of a greased 9"x13" pan. Place sausage over the bread.

🌿 Beat together eggs, milk, *Yoshida's®*, mustard and salt. Pour over the sausage and bread.

🌿 Cover and refrigerate overnight.

🌿 The next morning, preheat the oven to 325° F. In a small bowl, mix the mushroom soup with enough of the milk to make smooth. Pour over the casserole. Sprinkle on shredded cheese and bake for 1 hour.

Breakfast Burritos

makes eight

1/2 cup milk
8 eggs
8 flour tortillas
1 pound bulk pork sausage
1/2 cup diced green onions
1 cup shredded Cheddar cheese
3/4 cup *Yoshida's® Original Gourmet Sauce*
salsa *(optional accompaniment)*

🌿 In a medium–sized bowl, whisk together the milk and eggs. Heat a skillet over medium–low heat and scramble the eggs until just done. Transfer the eggs to a bowl, cover and set aside.

🌿 Turn oven to warm. Place tortillas on a plate, then cover with a damp dishcloth and place in oven to heat through.

🌿 In the same skillet used to scramble the eggs, brown the sausage and drain any excess liquid. Add 1/2 cup of the *Yoshida's®* and cook another 5 minutes. Set aside.

🌿 To assemble the burritos: place a warmed tortilla on a plate, layer on eggs, sausage, green onions and cheese at one end of the tortilla and drizzle sauce on generously. Fold the short end sides of the tortilla over the filling and roll up lengthwise into a burrito. Serve immediately with salsa, if desired.

Breakfast Burritos

Brunch

CREAMY CHEDDAR & POTATO CASSEROLE

serves eight to ten

1 1/2 pounds frozen O'Brien hash brown potatoes
1 can Cream of Chicken soup
1 teaspoon salt
1/4 cup melted butter
1/2 teaspoon pepper
1 pint nonfat sour cream
1/2 cup chopped onion
2 cups shredded Cheddar cheese
1/2 cup *Yoshida's®Hawaiian Sweet & Sour Sauce*

Topping:

2 cups crushed corn flakes
1/4 cups melted butter

❧ Slightly thaw potatoes and preheat oven to 350° F. In a large bowl combine all ingredients except for the topping and mix well. Spoon mixture into a 9"x13"x2" baking dish.

❧ In a small bowl combine the corn flakes and melted butter. Cover potato mixture with topping.

❧ Bake the casserole, uncovered, for 1 1/2 hours.

PINEAPPLE BRUNCH CASSEROLE

serves eight

1 cup Biscuit mix
1 cup milk
4 eggs, slightly beaten
6 tablespoons melted butter
1 teaspoon Dijon mustard
1/2 teaspoon onion powder
pinch ground nutmeg
1/2 cup *Yoshida's®Hawaiian Sweet & Sour Sauce*
4 ounces diced cooked ham
1 cup shredded Monterey Jack cheese
2 green onions, finely chopped
1 8 ounce can crushed pineapple, drained

❧ Preheat oven to 350° F.

❧ In a large mixing bowl combine Biscuit mix, milk, eggs, butter, mustard, onion powder, nutmeg and *Yoshida's®* until smooth. Stir in ham, cheese, onion and pineapple.

❧ Pour the mixture into a greased 9" pie plate. Bake for 35–40 minutes or until set. Serve hot.

MUSHROOM, SPINACH & TOMATO QUICHE

serves eight

1/2 cup chopped green onions
1/4 pound sliced mushrooms
1 clove fresh garlic, minced
2 tablespoons margarine
1 10 ounce package frozen chopped spinach
3 eggs, lightly beaten
1/4 cup *Yoshida's® Yakiniku Sauce*
3/4 cup cream
1 teaspoon salt

1 teaspoon basil
1/2 teaspoon celery salt
6 ounces shredded Swiss cheese
1–9" pie shell, unbaked
2 medium tomatoes, sliced
1 tablespoon Parmesan cheese
1 tablespoon dried bread crumbs

❧ Preheat the oven to 425°F.

❧ Sautè green onions, mushrooms and garlic in margarine until soft, about 5 minutes. Set aside.

❧ Thaw spinach and drain all liquid. Set aside.

❧ In a small bowl, combine eggs, *Yoshida's,®* cream and seasonings. Set aside.

❧ Put mushroom mixture, spinach and Swiss cheese into pie shell. Set the shell on a baking sheet and pour egg mixture into the shell. Arrange the tomato slices around the edge of the quiche. Bake for 15 minutes then turn the temperature down to 350°F. and bake another 20 minutes, remove.

❧ In a small bowl, mix together the Parmesan and bread crumbs. Sprinkle cheese mixture on top of the tomatoes and return the quiche to oven. Bake for another 10 minutes. Remove from oven and let stand 5 minutes before cutting.

Soups, Salads & Stews

Tex Mex Chicken Stew
28

Smokey Bean Chili
29

Beef Stew with Red Wine & Artichokes
29

Sweet & Sour Beef Stew
31

Sesame Chicken Salad
31

Chilled Steak Salad with Greens
34

Vegetable & Beef Soup
34

Hot Bacon Spinach Salad
36

Teriyaki Beef & Vegetable Stew
36

Asian Summer Salad
37

Chilled Creamy Chicken Salad
37

Chicken Salad with Sweet Bell Peppers
38

Rice & Vegetable Salad
38

Oriental Seafood Salad
39

Teriyaki-Orange Chicken Salad
39

Oriental Chicken Noodle Salad
42

Tex Mex Chicken Stew

TEX MEX CHICKEN STEW

serves four

3 pounds chicken pieces, bone–in
1 bay leaf
2 cups water
1 cup *Yoshida's® Spicy Wing & Rib Sauce*
1 15 ounce can black beans, drained
1 16 ounce can whole tomatoes
3 carrots, cut into 1/2" rounds
1 medium onion, chopped
2 tablespoons lemon juice

3 tablespoons fresh cilantro
2 tablespoons chili powder
1 1/2 teaspoons ground cumin
1 teaspoon marjoram
1 teaspoon salt
1/2 teaspoon ground pepper
3/4 cup uncooked rice
3 1/2 tablespoons cornstarch
1/4 cup water

❧ Place all ingredients except rice, cornstarch and 1/4 cup water in a crockpot. Cover and cook on low heat for 7–9 hours, or until chicken is very tender. Remove chicken from crockpot and set aside to cool. Discard bay leaf. When chicken is cool enough to handle, remove meat from bones and cut into bite–size pieces.

❧ Increase heat to high and stir in rice. Cover and cook for 30 minutes, or until rice is cooked. Return chicken to crockpot and stir well.

❧ Combine the cornstarch and water and stir into the stew. Reduce heat to low and stir to thicken. Garnish with extra cilantro before serving, if desired.

Soups/Stews

Smokey Bean Chili

serves six to eight

1/2 pound lean ground beef
3/4 pound bacon, chopped
1 cup rough chopped onion
1 cup *Yoshida's® Hawaiian Sweet & Sour Sauce*
1 cup *Yoshida's® Original Gourmet Sauce*
2 15 ounce cans pork and beans
1 tablespoon Liquid Smoke
1 15 ounce can kidney beans, drained
1 16 ounce can butter limas, drained
dash of ground pepper

❦ Brown ground beef over medium–high heat in a medium–sized skillet until cooked, about 5 minutes. Using a slotted spoon, transfer the beef to crockpot. Discard remaining liquid.

❦ Add bacon and onions to the same skillet and cook until just beginning to brown, about 5 minutes. Transfer drained mixture to crockpot with the beef.

❦ Add cans of beans and sauces to crockpot and stir well. Add the Liquid Smoke and season with pepper.

❦ Cook chili, covered, on low heat for 5–6 hours.

Beef Stew with Red Wine & Artichokes

serves four

2 pounds beef stew meat, cut in 1" cubes
salt & ground pepper *(to taste)*
2 tablespoons oil
3 celery stalks, cut diagonally in 1" pieces
1 large potato, cubed
1/2 cup chopped onion
1 8 ounce can tomato sauce
9 ounces fresh artichoke hearts
2 cloves fresh garlic, minced
1 tablespoon chopped parsley
1/4 cup dry red wine
1/4 cup *Yoshida's® Spicy Wing & Rib Sauce*

❦ Season beef with salt and pepper. Add oil to large skillet and over medium–high heat, cook the meat in batches until lightly browned, about 3–5 minutes. Transfer meat to a crockpot and add all remaining ingredients. Cover and cook on low for 7–9 hours, or until the meat is very tender.

❦ Serve the stew over rice or buttered noodles.

Beef Stew with Red Wine & Artichokes

Sweet & Sour Beef Stew

serves six

2 pounds beef stew meat, cut in 1" cubes
3/4 cup *Yoshida's® Original Gourmet Sauce*
1/4 cup *Yoshida's® Hawaiian Sweet & Sour Sauce*
1 15 ounce can Italian–style stewed tomatoes
1 medium onion, diced
2 cloves fresh garlic, minced
8 whole black peppercorns
2 cups baby carrots
3 medium potatoes, cut in 2" cubes
2 tablespoons cornstarch
3/4 cup water

❧ Marinate beef in 1/2 cup *Yoshida's® Original Gourmet Sauce* 8 hours or overnight.

❧ Turn crockpot temperature to high. When hot, add the beef and stir to sear all sides. Reduce heat to low and add remaining sauces, tomatoes, onion, garlic and peppercorns. Stir, cover and cook for 5 hours.

❧ Increase heat to medium–high. Add carrots and potatoes and continue cooking until tender, about 45 minutes. In a small bowl, mix the cornstarch and water to make a paste. Stir into the stew. Continue to stir until stew thickens, about 5 minutes.

Sesame Chicken Salad

serves six

1 1/2 pounds boneless, skinless chicken thighs
1 cup *Yoshida's® Original Gourmet Sauce*
iceberg lettuce
romaine lettuce
1 tablespoon oil
1 can sliced water chestnuts, drained
2/3 cup snow peas
1 cup red peppers, julienne sliced
1/3 cup thinly sliced green onions
toasted sesame seeds

❧ Place chicken thighs in a hot, medium–sized, non-stick skillet over medium–high heat and cook for 1 minute per side. Drain liquid from pan and add 3/4 cup *Yoshida's®*. Turn to coat chicken and cook uncovered for another 10–15 minutes until chicken is cooked through and sauce comes to a slow rolling boil and glazes chicken. Remove chicken from skillet and cut into strips. Wipe skillet clean.

❧ In a large bowl, tear lettuces into bite–size pieces and set aside.

❧ Heat oil in same skillet over medium–high heat and stir fry the water chestnuts, snow peas and red peppers until just beginning to soften, about 2 minutes. Add green onions and cook 1 more minute. Add chicken strips back to the skillet and stir fry another minute. Remove from heat.

❧ Toss chicken and vegetables with the lettuces. Drizzle remaining amount of *Yoshida's®* over the salad and sprinkle with sesame seeds.

Sesame Chicken Salad

Chilled Steak Salad with Greens

CHILLED STEAK SALAD WITH GREENS

served six

1/3 cup Yoshida's® Premium Steak Sauce
1/4 cup vegetable oil
2 tablespoons red wine vinegar
1 pound cooked sirloin steak, thinly sliced
1 medium onion, thinly sliced
1 medium tomato, cut in wedges
romaine lettuce
butter leaf lettuce
endive greens
bean sprouts
sesame seeds, toasted

🦋 In a medium–sized mixing bowl, whisk Yoshida's,® oil and vinegar until well blended. Add steak, onion and tomato. Mix well to coat all pieces. Cover and refrigerate at least 1 hour, stirring occasionally.

🦋 Tear the greens into bite–size pieces and portion onto plates with sprouts. Evenly divide the marinated meat mixture onto greens and sprinkle with sesame seeds.

VEGETABLE & BEEF SOUP

served four to six

1 pound lean ground beef
1 cup broccoli florets
1 cup diced carrots
1 cup cauliflower florets
1/2 cup pearl onions
1/2 package dry onion soup mix
1 cup water
2/3 cup Yoshida's® Classic Red Sweet & Sour Sauce
1 16 ounce can tomato sauce
salt and ground pepper *(to taste)*

🦋 Brown ground beef over medium–high heat in a large saucepan, about 5 minutes. Drain liquid from pan. Add the vegetables and cook until just beginning to soften, about 3 minutes. Sprinkle the soup mix over mixture and stir to coat. Pour in the water and stir.

🦋 Add Yoshida's® and tomato sauce to soup and stir well. Turn heat down to low and simmer soup about 20 minutes or until vegetables are tender.

🦋 Season to taste with salt and pepper.

Soups/Salads

Hot Bacon Spinach Salad

35

Hot Bacon Spinach Salad

serves four to six

1 cup *Yoshida's® Traditional Teriyaki Sauce*
1/2 cup rice vinegar
1/2 cup sugar
1/2 cup bacon pieces
2 cups mushrooms, sliced thin
1 cup sweet onion sliced thin & separated into rings
12 ounces fresh spinach leaves
2 tomatoes, wedged
3 hard boiled eggs, cut in half
croutons

❦ To make dressing: in a small saucepan, heat together sauce, vinegar and sugar.

❦ In a sautè pan brown the bacon, drain off grease and add mushrooms and onions. Cook mixture until the onions are soft, about 3 minutes. Add about 1/2 of the dressing to the pan. Set aside.

❦ Toss spinach with the remaining dressing, and portion onto plates. Spoon the bacon mixture over spinach and garnish plate with tomatoes, eggs and croutons.

Teriyaki Beef & Vegetable Stew

serves six

1 1/2 pounds chuck or round steak, cut in 1" cubes
3 tablespoons all purpose flour
2 cloves fresh garlic, minced
1/4 teaspoon gound pepper
1/2 cup *Yoshida's® Traditional Teriyaki Sauce*
1/4 cup *Yoshida's® Premium Steak Sauce*
2 cups fresh whole mushrooms
2 cups fresh pearl or stewing onions
1 cup baby carrots
3 medium potatoes, cut in 1" cubes
1 small zucchini squash, cut in 1" slices

❦ In a medium–sized bowl mix the beef with flour, garlic and pepper. Add seasoned beef to crockpot and pour in the *Yoshida®* sauces. Cook on low heat, covered, for 5 hours. Increase heat to high and add all the vegetables. Cook until tender, about 30 minutes.

❦ Serve stew over rice or buttered noodles.

Soups/Salads

Asian Summer Salad

serves four

2 medium tomatoes, cut in wedges

2 cups fresh bean sprouts

1 cup Tofu, or Mozzarella cheese, cut into 1/2" cubes

1 1/4 cups *Yoshida's® Quick & Easy Stir Fry Sauce*

1/4 cup rice vinegar

16 ounces mixed salad greens

1 sweet red bell pepper, julienne sliced

1 sweet yellow bell pepper, julienne sliced

1 medium sweet onion, sliced thin & separated into rings

roasted sesame seeds

❧ Marinate tomatoes, sprouts and Tofu in 1/4 cup *Yoshida's.®* Set aside.

❧ In medium-sized saucepan, bring the remaining sauce and vinegar almost to a simmer and add peppers and onions. Let steep 5 minutes.

❧ Divide greens between four salad plates. Top with equal portions of tomatoes, sprouts and Tofu. Spoon the heated peppers and onions around the greens. Dress the greens with additional sauce from pan if desired. Garnish with sesame seeds.

Chilled Creamy Chicken Salad

serves four

3 tablespoons butter

3 boneless, skinless chicken breasts

1/4 teaspoon salt

1/4 teaspoon ground pepper

1/4 cup thinly sliced celery

1/4 cup thinly sliced green onions

1/4 cup chopped fresh parsley

1/4 cup *Yoshida's® Quick & Easy Stir Fry*

1/4 cup lite sour cream

2 tablespoons mayonnaise

1/2 teaspoon mustard seed

2 tablespoons Dijon mustard

1 tablespoon lemon juice

8 lettuce leaves

1 cup cherry tomato halves

❧ In a medium-sized skillet, melt butter and sautè the chicken until lightly browned and chicken is cooked through, about 3 minutes per side. Season chicken with salt and pepper, remove from pan and set aside to chill in refrigerator.

❧ When the chicken is cold, cut into bite-size pieces and place in a medium-sized bowl. Add the celery, onions and parsley to the chicken. Toss well.

❧ In a small bowl, stir together *Yoshida's,®* sour cream, mayonnaise, mustard seed, mustard and lemon juice. Add to the chicken mixture and blend well. Chill.

❧ Arrange lettuce leaves on a platter or plates. Top with chicken salad and garnish with tomatoes.

Salads

Chicken Salad with Sweet Bell Peppers

serves four

1/3 cup sake or white wine
3 boneless, skinless chicken breasts
1 red bell pepper, julienne sliced
1 green bell pepper, julienne sliced
1 yellow bell pepper, julienne sliced
1/2 Bermuda onion, thinly sliced
1 cup *Yoshida's*® *Quick & Easy Stir Fry Sauce*

4 ounces spinach leaves
4 Roma tomatoes, cut in wedges
1/4 cup sliced green onions
toasted sesame seeds

❧ In a small saucepan, heat sake or wine over medium–low heat and poach the chicken until cooked through, about 5–10 minutes.

❧ Remove chicken from liquid and chill.

❧ In a medium–sized bowl toss bell peppers and onions with 2/3 cup *Yoshida's*® and chill 30 minutes. When chicken is cold, shred into pieces and marinate in remaining 1/3 cup *Yoshida's.*® Chill 30 minutes.

❧ When ready to serve, line plates with spinach leaves and portion vegetables on top. Center chicken on the vegetables. Garnish the salad with tomato wedges and sprinkle green onions and sesame seeds over salad.

Rice & Vegetable Salad

serves six

2 cups *Yoshida's*® *Quick & Easy Stir Fry Sauce*
1 cup julienne sliced red bell peppers
1 cup julienne sliced green bell peppers
1/2 cup sliced carrots
1/2 cup sliced celery
(or 3 cups of any mixed vegetables–broccoli, cauliflower, onions, mushrooms etc.)
3 cups cooked white rice, chilled
1/2 cup chopped green onions
2 tablespoons toasted sesame seeds

❧ In a large bowl, mix 1 cup of *Yoshida's*® with vegetables and chill.

❧ In another bowl, toss remaining *Yoshida's*® with rice, green onions and 1 1/2 tablespoons sesame seeds.

❧ To serve, spread rice out on a platter and spoon on the vegetables. Sprinkle with remaining 1/2 tablespoon sesame seeds. Serve immediately.

Salads

Oriental Seafood Salad

serves four as an entree

1 cup *Yoshida's® Original Gourmet Sauce*
1/2 cup rice vinegar
2 tablespoons sesame oil
1/2 pound cooked shrimp, chilled
1/2 pound cooked scallops, chilled
1/2 pound cooked whitefish *(halibut is best)*, 2" pieces, chilled
1 cup sliced mushrooms
1 15 ounce can bamboo shoots, drained
1/2 cup cubed and cooked Tofu or Mozzarella cheese
1 pound bag mixed salad greens

❧ Make dressing by whisking the *Yoshida's®* with the vinegar and sesame oil. Set aside.

❧ In a medium–sized bowl, place chilled seafood with mushrooms, bamboo shoots and Tofu. Pour half of the dressing over the mixture and very gently combine.

❧ In a large salad bowl, toss salad greens with remaining dressing and transfer to a serving platter. Spoon the seafood mixture over greens and serve immediately.

Teriyaki–Orange Chicken Salad

serves four

1/2 cup *Yoshida's® Traditional Teriyaki Sauce*
1/4 cup orange juice
dash of cayenne pepper
4 chicken breast halves
1 package ramen–type noodles
4–5 cups greens *(lettuce, spinach or cabbage)*
1 cup mandarin orange segments
cilantro (garnish)

❧ Mix *Yoshida's®* orange juice and cayenne pepper together in a non–metal dish.

❧ Pierce the chicken all over with a fork and marinate in sauce, covered, in the refrigerator 10–15 minutes or up to 24 hours.

❧ Heat a skillet over medium heat and drain chicken from marinade. Cook chicken until just done, about 5 minutes per side.

❧ Toast ramen noodles under broiler (do not use seasoning packet) while chicken is cooking. Stir them frequently to prevent burning.

❧ To assemble salad: spread a layer of noodles onto 4 plates. Next, divide cleaned greens on top of the noodles. Slice the cooked chicken into 1/2" thick pieces and arrange them on top of the greens. Spread the mandarin oranges around the chicken. Spoon additional sauce over chicken slices. Garnish with cilantro.

Teriyaki–Orange Chicken Salad

Oriental Chicken Noodle Salad

41

ORIENTAL CHICKEN NOODLE SALAD

served six

Oriental Noodles, *(7.5 ounce package of Yakisoba)*
1 teaspoon salad oil
4 boneless, skinless chicken breasts or thighs
1/4 cup *Yoshida's® Original Gourmet Sauce*
2 cups shredded Napa cabbage or Bok Choy
3/4 cup *Yoshida's® Quick & Easy Stir Fry Sauce*
1 carrot, julienne sliced
1/4 Daikon radish, julienne sliced
1/2 cup broccoli florets
3/4 cup fresh cilantro leaves *(garnish)*

❧ Cook noodles, toss with the oil and chill.

❧ In a medium–sized skillet over medium–high heat, cook chicken until golden on each side, about 1 minute per side. Drain liquid from pan, add *Yoshida's® Original Gourmet Sauce*, bring sauce to a simmer and reduce heat to low. Simmer uncovered, turning chicken occasionally, until cooked through and sauce thickens to a glaze. Remove chicken from skillet and set aside. When cooled, cut in 1/4" slices.

❧ In a small bowl, marinate the cabbage in 1/4 cup *Yoshida's® Quick & Easy Stir Fry Sauce*, chill. In another bowl, add vegetables and 1/4 cup of the remaining sauce and chill. Add the last 1/4 cup sauce to the noodles and toss. Chill.

❧ To assemble the salad, set each plate with a layer of cabbage and twirl a portion of noodles onto cabbage. Dress the outer edge of the cabbage with the vegetables. Fan out the chicken slices on top of the noodles and garnish with cilantro.

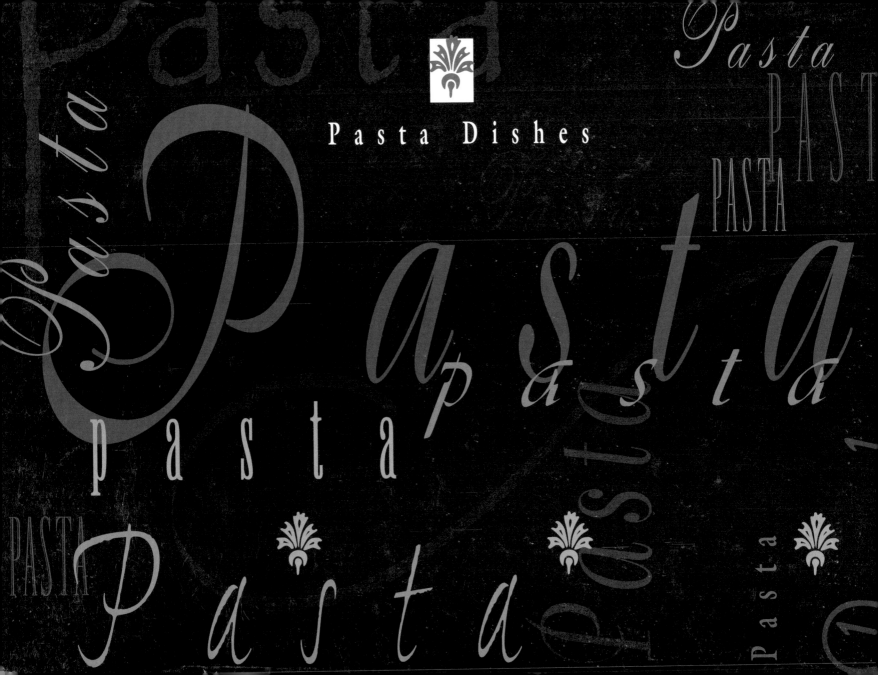

Pasta Dishes

Outstanding Pasta Dish
43

Marinated Chicken Pasta Salad
43

Crab & Cheese Roll-ups
46

Tangy Tomato Pasta Sauce
47

Gourmet Sautè Italiano
47

Hawaiian Lasagna
49

Hearty Autumn Fettuccini
49

Baked Cheese & Vegetable Pasta
50

OUTSTANDING PASTA DISH

serves four

8 ounces linguini
1 red bell pepper, julienne sliced
1 yellow squash, julienne sliced
1 medium red onion, sliced thinly
1 green bell pepper, julienne sliced
1/2 cup *Yoshida's® Original Gourmet Sauce*
4 tablespoons virgin olive oil
salt & pepper (to taste)

❧ Cook pasta according to package directions, drain and place in serving bowl. Add all vegetables to the pasta and toss with *Yoshida's®* and olive oil. Season to taste with salt and pepper.

❧ *This dish is great served hot or cold.*

———————

Marvin Rosenblum   Boca Raton, FL

MARINATED CHICKEN PASTA SALAD

serves four

1 pound boneless, skinless chicken thighs
1 cup nonfat yogurt
2 tablespoons Dijon mustard
2 1/4 cups *Yoshida's® Original Gourmet Sauce*
1 tablespoon fresh garlic, minced
8 ounces cooked and cooled bow tie pasta
3 plum tomatoes, cut lengthwise, halved and sliced
1/2 cup thinly sliced carrot
1 small can sliced olives, drained
2 green onions, sliced diagonally into 1/2" pieces

❧ Cut chicken into bite–size pieces and marinate in 2 cups *Yoshida's®*. Refrigerate for at least 1 hour. Broil or microwave chicken until done. Set aside to cool.

❧ In a medium–sized bowl whisk the yogurt, mustard, remaining *Yoshida's®* and minced garlic. Add the pasta, cooled chicken, tomatoes, carrots, olives and green onions and mix well.

❧ Chill, covered in the refrigerator for 1 hour before serving.

Pasta

Marinated Chicken Pasta Salad

44

Crab & Cheese Roll–Ups

CRAB & CHEESE ROLL-UPS

serves four to six

9 lasagna noodles

Filling:

1 pound fresh or immitation crab chunks
1 cup cottage cheese
1/4 cup grated Parmesan cheese
3 eggs, lightly beaten
1 tablespoon chopped fresh parsley
1/2 teaspoon onion powder
1 1/2 cups *Yoshida's® Hawaiian Sweet & Sour Sauce*

Garnish:

2 tablespoons grated Parmesan cheese
1 tablespoon chopped fresh parsley

- Cook the lasagna noodles as directed on the package. Rinse in cold water, drain and set aside.
- Preheat the oven to 375° F.
- Reserving 1 cup *Yoshida's®*, mix all filling ingredients together.
- To assemble, spread 1/3 cup of the filling on the noodle and roll up tightly. Place each roll–up seam–side down in a 9" baking pan. Continue this process until all noodles are placed snugly together in the pan. Pour the remaining *Yoshida's®* evenly over the roll–ups.
- Bake on the middle rack of the oven for 30 minutes. Serve hot and garnish with the Parmesan and parsley.

Pasta

Tangy Tomato Pasta Sauce

serves four to six

1 1/2 pounds lean ground beef
5 cloves fresh garlic, minced
4–5 green onions, thinly sliced
1 large onion, finely chopped
1 teaspoon ground pepper
1/3 cup sherry
1 cup *Yoshida's®Hawaiian Sweet & Sour Sauce*
1 15 ounce can tomato sauce
12 ounces cooked spaghetti noodles

❧ Cook the ground beef in a medium–sized skillet over medium–high heat until browned, about 5 minutes. Drain liquid from pan.

❧ Add garlic and onions to the meat and cook another 3 minutes or until onions start to soften. Season with pepper and turn the heat down to medium.

❧ Add sherry, *Yoshida's®*and tomato sauce. Stir and simmer 5 minutes.

❧ Serve hot over noodles.

Shirley Vornali   Petaluma, CA

Gourmet Sautè Italiano

serves six

5 Italian sausage links, sliced 1/3 " thick
1 tablespoon olive oil
1 celery stalk, thinly sliced
1 medium red onion, thinly sliced
1 red bell pepper, julienne sliced
6 cloves fresh garlic, minced
1 teaspoon oregano
1 teaspoon basil
1/2 teaspoon black pepper
1/2 cup *Yoshida's®Original Gourmet Sauce*

6 servings cooked linguini
1/4 cup grated
　　Parmesan cheese
6 sprigs fresh parsley

❧ In a large skillet over medium heat, cook sausages until lightly browned, about 5 minutes. Remove sausages to a plate lined with a paper towel. Drain grease from skillet. Return skillet to heat and sauté celery, red onion, bell pepper and garlic in olive oil 3 minutes or until tender. Season the vegetables with oregano, basil and pepper. Add *Yoshida's®*

❧ Return the sausage to the skillet and simmer the mixture about 3 minutes until heated through.

❧ Serve over hot linguini and garnish with Parmesan cheese and parsley.

Alice Volkens   Jackson, N.J.

Gourmet Sautè Italiano

Pasta

HAWAIIAN LASAGNA

serves six to eight

1/2 cup *Yoshida's® Hawaiian Sweet & Sour Sauce*

1 cup tomato sauce

2 cups cooked ham or Canadian bacon, cubed

2 cups pineapple chunks

1/4 cup diced green bell peppers

32 ounces Ricotta cheese, *(4 cups)*

3 cups shredded Mozzarella cheese

1 cup grated Parmesan cheese

4 fresh lasagna sheets

❧ Preheat oven to 375° F.

❧ In a small saucepan, warm sauces together over low heat until hot, not boiling. Set aside.

❧ In a large skillet, cook ham, pineapple and green peppers over medium heat until hot and some liquid is released, about 5 minutes. Remove from heat and set aside.

❧ In a 9"x13" pan, coat bottom of pan with a thin layer of sauce. Place a lasagna sheet over the sauce and cover with another thin layer of sauce. Layer 1/4 of the Ricotta cheese, 1/4 of the ham mixture, 1/4 of the Mozzarella and add a thin layer of sauce. Repeat this layering 3 more times and finish the top layer with remaining sauce and Parmesan cheese.

❧ Cover with foil and bake for 35–40 minutes. Remove foil and let sit 10 minutes before slicing.

HEARTY AUTUMN FETTUCCINI

serves six

2 cups sliced varietal squash

2 cups sliced mushrooms

1 3/4 cup *Yoshida's® Quick & Easy Stir Fry Sauce*

1 cup tomato ketchup

16 ounces cooked fettuccini

2 cups, 1/2" cubes, Mozzarella cheese

1/2 cup grated Parmesan cheese

fresh cilantro sprigs *(garnish)*

❧ In a large skillet, sautè squash and mushrooms over medium–high heat for 2 minutes or until tender. Add *Yoshida's®* and ketchup to skillet and stir to mix. Bring sauce to a simmer then remove from heat.

❧ Warm a platter in the oven. Prior to serving, place pasta on warm platter. Add the Mozzarella cheese to sauce and vegetables in the skillet and pour over the pasta.

❧ Garnish with Parmesan and cilantro.

BAKED CHEESE & VEGETABLE PASTA

serves four to six

12 ounces dried fettuccini noodles
2 tablespoons butter
2 carrots, sliced in 1/4 " rounds
1 cup broccoli florets
1 clove fresh garlic, minced
2 zucchinis, sliced into 1/4" rounds
1/2 cup thinly sliced red bell pepper
1 1/2 cups thinly sliced mushrooms
4 green onions, thinly sliced

1/2 teaspoon dried basil
1/2 teaspoon ground pepper
1 cup grated Mozzarella cheese
1 cup cream
3/4 cup *Yoshida's*® *Yakiniku Sauce*
3/4 cup grated Parmesan cheese

❧ Preheat oven to 375° F.

❧ Cook fettuccini noodles according to package directions, drain and place in large bowl.

❧ In a medium–sized sautè pan, melt half the butter and sautè the carrots until halfway tender. Add the broccoli florets and finish cooking till both are just tender. Add to noodles.

❧ To the same pan, add the rest of the butter and melt. Add the garlic and cook one minute.

❧ Add the zucchini and sautè one minute. Add peppers, mushrooms and onions. Continue cooking a few minutes until the vegetables are just tender. Add these vegetables to the pasta.

❧ Add the seasonings and Mozzarella to the pasta and toss. Pour cream and *Yoshida's*® over the mixture and stir together gently.

❧ Pour into a 4–quart casserole dish and bake for 15 minutes or until bubbly.

❧ Sprinkle with Parmesan cheese and serve immediately.

Pasta

Side Dishes

Wingin' Green Beans
52

Buttery Topped Tomatoes
52

Sweet Broccoli & Onion Augratin
53

Spanish Style Cauliflower
53

Chinese-Style Fried Rice
54

Sweet & Sour Slow Cooked Beans
54

Bacon Corn Bake
56

Teriyaki Twice Baked Potatoes
56

Hot & Smokey Baked Beans
58

Teriyaki Mushrooms & Tomatoes
58

Wingin' Green Beans

WINGIN' GREEN BEANS
serves four

2 tablespoons butter or margarine
1/2 red onion, julienne sliced
4 mushrooms, sliced
1 cup fresh cut green beans
1 cup fresh waxed beans
1/4 cup *Yoshida's® Spicy Wing & Rib Sauce*
1/4 cup whole cashew nuts, toasted

Melt butter in a large skillet over medium heat until bubbling.

Add onions, mushrooms and beans. Sautè until just tender, about 3 minutes. Lower heat and add *Yoshida's®.* Stir to coat and cook until heated through, about 2 minutes.

Serve beans on a platter and sprinkle with the cashews.

BUTTERY TOPPED TOMATOES
serves four

2 tablespoons melted butter
1/3 cup finely crushed buttery crackers
1/2 cup shredded Cheddar cheese
1 tablespoon chopped fresh parsley
2 tablespoons butter or margarine
1/4 teaspoon caraway seed
1/4 teaspoon salt
pinch of pepper
1 tablespoon chopped onion
4 tablespoons *Yoshida's® Yakiniku Sauce*
2 large ripe tomatoes, cut into 10 wedges

In a small bowl, stir together melted butter, crushed crackers, cheese and parsley. Set aside.

In a large skillet, melt 2 tablespoons butter. Stir in caraway seed, salt, pepper, onion and *Yoshida's®.* Cook for 2–3 minutes. Add tomatoes, cover and cook over medium heat stirring occasionally, until heated through. Sprinkle with cheese mixture. Cover and let stand 1 minute. Serve immediately.

Sweet Broccoli & Onion Augratin

serves six to eight

Cheese Sauce:

2 tablespoons butter
2 tablespoons flour
1/2 teaspoon salt
1/4 teaspoon rosemary
1/4 teaspoon pepper
1/4 cup *Yoshida's® Classic Red Sweet & Sour Sauce*
1 1/2 cups milk, warmed
1 cup shredded Swiss cheese
4 cups broccoli florets
1 medium onion, chopped

Topping:

1 cup bread crumbs
1/3 cup melted butter
1/4 cup fresh chopped parsley

❧ Heat oven to 350° F.

❧ In a medium–sized saucepan, melt butter over medium–low heat until foaming. Stir in flour, salt, rosemary and pepper. Add *Yoshida's®* and milk and continue stirring until the sauce comes to a boil and is thickened. Stir in cheese until mixture is smooth. Remove from heat and set aside.

❧ In a small bowl, combine the topping ingredients and set aside.

❧ Place broccoli and onion in a greased, shallow casserole dish. Pour cheese sauce over the vegetables and sprinkle on the topping.

❧ Bake the casserole for 30–40 minutes.

Spanish Style Cauliflower

serves eight

1 head cauliflower
1/4 cup melted butter or margarine
1/2 teaspoon pepper
1/2 teaspoon salt
3/4 cup cracker crumbs
1/2 cup diced green peppers
1 16 ounce can tomatoes
3/4 cup *Yoshida's® Hawaiian Sweet & Sour Sauce*
1 medium onion, chopped
1 1/2 cups shredded Cheddar cheese

❧ Preheat oven to 350° F.

❧ Rinse cauliflower and remove outer leaves. Break or cut into florets and steam for about 5 minutes (or cook in a small amount of salted water), drain. Combine butter, pepper, salt and cracker crumbs in large bowl. Add the bell peppers, tomatoes, *Yoshida's®* onion, 1 1/4 cup cheese and cauliflower. Toss well. Pour mixture into a 2 quart casserole dish and top with remaining cheese.

❧ Bake for 1 hour. Serve hot.

Chinese-Style Fried Rice
serves eight

3 eggs
2 tablespoons water
4 strips bacon, diced
2 cups thinly sliced green onions, green tops reserved
1 tablespoon freshly grated ginger root
3 cloves fresh garlic, minced
7 cups cooked rice
1/2 cup white table wine
1/2 cup *Yoshida's® Original Gourmet Sauce*
3/4 cup green onion tops, chopped, save for garnish

❧ In a small bowl, whip eggs with water and pour into a hot, 12" non–stick skillet over medium heat. Cover and cook until firm, about 3 minutes. Turn eggs onto cutting board and cut into 1/4" x 3" strips, set aside.

❧ Brown bacon over medium heat in a large frying pan. Add green onions, ginger and garlic to the bacon and sautè for 1 minute. Add the rice, wine and *Yoshida's.®* Continue to cook until mixture is heated through, about 3–5 minutes. Return egg to the rice and stir to mix.

❧ Serve with the green onions as garnish.

Sweet & Sour Slow Cooked Beans
serves eight to ten

8 bacon slices, cut in 1/2" pieces
1 tablespoon soy sauce
1 medium onion, chopped
2 15 ounce cans kidney beans, drained
1 clove fresh garlic, minced
1 1/2 cups *Yoshida's® Hawaiian Sweet & Sour Sauce*
2 16 ounce cans baked beans
1 tablespoon prepared mustard
2 17 ounce cans lima beans, drained

❧ Cook bacon over medium heat, remove and drain on paper towel.

❧ Reserve 3 tablespoons of bacon drippings and add to crockpot.

❧ Add all remaining ingredients to crockpot. Stir well to blend, cover and cook on low for 7–8 hours or overnight. You could also cook the beans on high for 2–3 hours.

Bacon Corn Bake

Bacon Corn Bake

serves eight

6 slices bacon, cut in small pieces
1/2 cup chopped onion
2 tablespoons flour
1/2 teaspoon salt
1/2 teaspoon pepper
1 clove fresh garlic, minced

1/4 cup *Yoshida's® Yakiniku Sauce*
1 cup lite sour cream
2 packages frozen whole kernel corn
1 tablespoon chopped fresh parsley
1 tablespoon chopped fresh chives

❧ Heat oven to 350°F.

❧ In a medium–sized skillet, cook bacon over medium heat until partially cooked. Add onion and continue cooking until the bacon is browned and onion is soft, about 5 minutes. Remove bacon and onion with a slotted spoon and set aside. Pour off all remaining liquid in skillet except for 1 tablespoon.

❧ Reheat the skillet over medium heat and add the flour, salt, pepper and garlic. Stir well to combine and cook the roux until smooth and bubbly, about 3 minutes. Stir in the *Yoshida's,®* sour cream, corn and remaining bacon and onion mixture.

❧ Pour mixture into a casserole dish and bake for 25–30 minutes. Sprinkle with parsley and chives. Serve warm.

Teriyaki Twice Baked Potatoes

makes four

4 large baking potatoes
1 cup *Yoshida's® Original Gourmet Sauce*
1/4 cup *Yoshida's® Traditional Teriyaki Sauce*
1/2 cup chopped and cooked bacon or sausage
3/4 cup chopped green onions
1/2 cup shredded Cheddar cheese
1/4 cup sour cream
1 egg

❧ Preheat the oven to 375°F.

❧ Scrub potatoes, prick several times with a fork and bake for about 1 hour or until tender when pierced with a fork. Raise the oven temperature to 400°F.

❧ Let potatoes cool slightly, slice off the tops lengthwise and carefully scoop out the pulp leaving 1/4" still attached to the skins. Place the pulp into a medium–sized bowl and mash.

❧ Mix in the sauces, bacon or sausage, onions, cheese, sour cream and egg.

❧ Divide the filling equally among the shells, mounding the filling slightly. Place potatoes on a baking sheet and place on the middle shelf of the oven. Bake for 20 minutes or until filling is hot.

❧ Serve immediately.

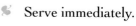

Hot & Smokey Baked Beans

Hot & Smokey Baked Beans

serves ten to fourteen

3 1/2 cups dried white beans *(soak according to pkg)*
1 smoked ham hock, 4 ounces
3 1/2 teaspoons salt
2 cups finely chopped onions
1 1/2 cups *Yoshida's® Spicy Wing & Rib Sauce*
1 1/2 cups tomato–based hot salsa
1/3 cup brown sugar, firmly packed
1/4 cup Dijon mustard
1/4 cup light molasses
2 tablespoons chopped cilantro, for garnish

❧ Place beans in a heavy, oven–proof pot and cover with cold water. Bring pot to a boil and simmer the beans for 5 minutes. Remove pot from heat. Let sit for 1 hour covered. Drain the beans, cover again with cold water and add ham hock to the pot. Bring pot to a boil, reduce heat to low and simmer for 20 minutes. Add 2 teaspoons salt and simmer another 20 minutes, stirring occasionally. Remove ham hock and reserve. Drain beans, reserving 1 1/2 cups of the liquid.

❧ Preheat the oven to 350° F.

❧ Return beans to pot and add remaining ingredients, mixing well. Place ham hock in center of the beans, cover and bake on center rack for 1 hour. Uncover pot, bake another 40 minutes until the bean mixture is very thick, stirring occasionally. Remove the ham hock and discard. Serve the beans with cilantro as garnish.

Teriyaki Mushrooms & Tomatoes

serves four

2 cups *Yoshida's® Traditional Teriyaki Sauce*
1 cup rice vinegar
2 tablespoons sugar
4 cups whole mushrooms
6 large tomatoes, cut in wedges
1/2 cup thinly sliced sweet red onions
1 head green or red leaf lettuce

❧ In a large saucepan, stir together 1 1/2 cups *Yoshida's,®* vinegar and sugar over medium heat. When hot, add mushrooms and onions. Reduce heat to low and cook until mushrooms are tender, about 10 minutes. Drain and chill.

❧ In a medium–sized bowl, mix tomatoes with remaining 1/2 cup *Yoshida's.®* Cover and refrigerate for 1 hour.

❧ Drain tomatoes and mix with mushrooms and onions. Arrange lettuce on a platter or plates and spoon vegetable mixture over lettuce. Serve immediately.

PORK DISHES
59-70

Pork Tenderloin with Mushroom Sauce
Hawaiian Glazed Baked Ham
Gourmet Pork Chops
Garlic Hawaiian Pork Chops
Teriyaki Roast Pork Tenderloin
Pork Tenderloin with Snow Peas
Yoshida's® Pork Roast
Pork Rib Sandwich
"East Meets West" Pork Chops
Hawaiian Style Pizza
Sweet Baby Back Ribs
Country Style Pork Ribs
Hawaiian Style Sweet & Sour Kielbasa

BEEF DISHES
71-80

Peppers Stuffed with Beef & Cheddar
Cheese Steak Sandwich
Beef Stroganoff
Stuffed Cabbage Rolls
Italian–Style Meatloaf
Country Meatloaf & Vegetables
Beef Pot Roast
Beef Roast with Horseradish
Stir Fry Broccoli with Beef
Traditional Yakiniku Beef

BEEF DISHES (CONT.)
81-85

Teriyaki Burgers
Sloppy Joes
Savory Beef Pot Pie
"Korokei" Beef
Jerky

POULTRY DISHES
86-101

Mandarin Orange Chicken
Sesame Chicken
Lemon & Garlic Cornish Game Hens
Mushroom & Cheese Stuffed Chicken
Chicken Fajitas
Chicken Burritos
Spicy Wine Poached Chicken
Chicken & Spinach Pie with Buttermilk Biscuits
Gourmet BBQ Chicken
Demo Chicken
Grilled Chicken & Vegetables
Cashew Chicken
Roast Gourmet Turkey Breast
Hawaiian Sweet & Sour Turkey
Teriyaki Chicken Sandwich
Creamy Chicken Stuffed Pitas
Sweet & Sour Chicken
Shirley Temple Chicken Wings
Chicken Calzones
Lemon & Ginger Chicken with Pineapple

FISH & SEAFOOD DISHES
102-109

Lightly Smoked & Grilled Salmon
Fish Fillets with Pineapple Sauce
Broiled Halibut
Seared Ahi Tuna Steaks
Glazed Seafood Medley in Puff Pastry
Shrimp Kabobs
Teriyaki Fish Kabobs
Crab Cheese Delight
Sweet & Sour Shrimp Stir Fry

VEGETARIAN DISHES
110-114

Vegetable Strudel
Savory Vegetable Pizza
Versatile Vegetable Delight
Vegetable Shish–Kabobs

SPECIALTY DISHES
115-118

Roast Lamb Chops with Apricots & Honey
Veal Stroganoff
Roast Lamb with Garlic, Rosemary & Lemon
Venison with Sour Cream & Mushrooms

Pork Tenderloin with Mushroom Sauce

Pork Tenderloin with Mushroom Sauce

serves six

1 pork tenderloin
1 1/2 cups *Yoshida's® Original Gourmet Sauce*
mushroom sauce

Mushroom Sauce:

2 tablespoons butter or margarine
few drops sesame oil
1 clove fresh garlic, minced
9 mushrooms, sliced *(any variety)*
1/4 cup white wine
1/8 cup *Yoshida's® Original Gourmet Sauce*

❧ Marinate the pork in 1 1/2 cups *Yoshida's®* at least 6 hours or overnight. (A heavy plastic zip lock bag works well.)

❧ Preheat oven to 325° F. Place pork on a baking sheet on middle rack of oven. Bake for 1–1 1/2 hours or until a meat thermometer registers 160° F.

❧ Remove pork from oven and set aside while making the sauce. (Tent roast with a piece of foil to keep warm.)

❧ To make the sauce, melt butter and oil in a hot skillet over medium heat and sauté garlic and mushrooms about 3 minutes or until tender. Pour in wine and cook 1 minute. Add *Yoshida's®* and cook another 2–3 minutes. Remove skillet from heat.

❧ To serve, slice pork and place on a platter or plates and serve the mushroom sauce around the pork.

Lori Harper   Tucson, AZ

Hawaiian Glazed Baked Ham

serves twelve to sixteen

4–5 pounds fully cooked boneless cured ham
3 cups *Yoshida's® Hawaiian Sweet & Sour Sauce*
1 can pineapple rings, drained

❧ Preheat oven to 350° F.

❧ Place the ham in a 9"x13" baking pan and pour 2 cups of *Yoshida's®* over ham. Bake in the lower third of the oven for 1–1 1/2 hours, basting every 15 minutes with pan juices, or until heated through. During the last half hour of cooking time, place pineapple rings decoratively over the top. Serve the carved ham with remaining 1 cup of sauce, heated.

Pork

Gourmet Pork Chops

serves four

salt & pepper *(to taste)*
1/4 cup all purpose flour
4 pork loin chops, 1" thick
3 tablespoons peanut oil
1/2 cup finely chopped onion
1 clove fresh garlic, minced

1/2 pound fresh mushrooms, sliced
1/2 cup dry white wine
1 cup chicken stock
1/4 cup *Yoshida's® Original Gourmet Sauce*
1/4 teaspoon dried thyme
1 bay leaf

❦ Preheat oven to 350° F.

❦ Combine salt and pepper with the flour in a plastic bag. Add pork chops one by one and shake to coat well. Heat a skillet over medium heat and add oil.

❦ Brown the pork chops, about 2 minutes per side, drain on paper towels. Place chops in a casserole dish, set aside.

❦ In same skillet, add the onion, garlic and mushrooms. Sautè until tender, about 5 minutes.

❦ Pour in the wine and scrape up all bits left from browning. Add chicken stock, *Yoshida's,®* thyme and bay leaf to the pan. Simmer 1 minute and pour over pork chops.

❦ Cover and bake 45 minutes or until pork is tender. Remove bay leaf and serve.

Garlic Hawaiian Pork Chops

serves four

4 pork chops
1 cup flour
1 tablespoon olive oil
garlic salt *(to taste)*
1/2 cup *Yoshida's® Hawaiian Sweet & Sour Sauce*
pepper *(to taste)*

❦ Preheat oven to 325° F.

❦ Coat pork chops in flour. Heat olive oil in a skillet over medium-high heat and brown meat approximately 2 minutes per side. Sprinkle each side with garlic salt.

❦ Place pork chops in a 9"x13" baking dish and spoon 2 tablespoons of *Yoshida's®* over each chop. Sprinkle with pepper.

❦ Bake for about 45 minutes or until the juices run clear (baking time will vary depending on thickness.)

Garlic Hawaiian Pork Chops

Teriyaki Roast Pork Tenderloin

63

Pork

Teriyaki Roast Pork Tenderloin

serves eight

Pork Tenderloin with Snow Peas

serves four

2 whole pork tenderloins
1 1/2 cups *Yoshida's® Traditional Teriyaki Sauce*
4 medium potatoes, peeled & quartered
1/2 pound seasonal onions, *(Bermuda's etc.)* peeled and halved
4 large carrots, peeled & halved

1 pound pork loin
1 cup *Yoshida's® Original Gourmet Sauce*
4–6 scallions
1 large sweet red pepper, julienne strips
2 teaspoons oil
1 cup Chinese pea pods
1 1/2 cups steamed white rice

❧ Marinate pork in *Yoshida's®* for a minimum of 1 hour.

❧ Preheat oven to 375˚ F. Remove tenderloins from marinade, reserving marinade. In an oiled skillet heated over medium–high heat, sear tenderloins by browning them on all sides.

❧ Transfer tenderloins to a roasting pan. Add vegetables and bake in the oven for about 30–45 minutes or to desired doneness. Baste meat with reserve marinade occasionally while cooking.

❧ Slice tenderloins and serve with roasted vegetables.

❧ Cut the pork loin into strips about 1/4"x2" and marinate in *Yoshida's®* for 30 minutes in the refrigerator.

❧ Heat a wok or skillet and sautè scallions and peppers in oil briefly, about 1 minute.

❧ Add snow peas and pork. Sautè until pork is thoroughly cooked, about 3 minutes.

❧ Serve over rice.

Thecla McPartland   Huntington, NY

Yoshida's Pork Roast

serves eight

3 pounds boneless pork shoulder roast
1 1/2 cups *Yoshida's® Original Gourmet Sauce*
1 1/2 teaspoons Liquid Smoke

❧ Slice the pork in half lengthwise and place in a large zip lock bag. Combine 1 cup of *Yoshida's®* and Liquid Smoke. Pour over the pork, seal and marinate 8 hours or overnight, turning bag occasionally.

❧ Preheat oven to 350° F.

❧ Remove pork from marinade. Place in a shallow baking pan and cover. Bake for 1 hour, basting with the remaining 1/2 cup sauce. Uncover, turn the pork over, baste again and continue cooking another hour, or until very tender.

Pork Rib Sandwich

serves six

2–4 pounds boneless country style pork ribs
1 1/2 cups white vinegar
3 cups *Yoshida's® Original Gourmet Sauce*
1/4 cup finely chopped onions
6 French rolls

❧ Place ribs in a glass or ceramic dish and pour vinegar and 1 cup *Yoshida's®* over them.

❧ Cover and marinate in refrigerator for 8 hours. After 8 hours, pour off marinade and discard. Dry the ribs gently with paper towels and place in a roasting pan.

❧ Preheat oven to 300 °F.

❧ Mix the remaining sauce with onions and pour over ribs, turning to coat. Cover pan and bake on middle rack of oven for 1 hour. Remove lid from pan and bake another hour until ribs are very tender.

❧ Remove pan from oven and let sit a few minutes to cool. Shred meat and serve on French rolls with the sauce.

Denice Shipp Sacramento, CA

"East Meets West" Pork Chops

serves four

4 boneless pork chops
2 tablespoons vegetable oil
1 can Cream of Mushroom soup
1 soup can of water
3/4 cup *Yoshida's® Original Gourmet Sauce*
1/4 teaspoon garlic powder
2 cups broccoli florets, pre–cooked
2 cups cooked white rice
2 teaspoons toasted sesame seeds
1/4 teaspoon ground pepper

❧ Add oil to a medium–sized skillet and brown pork chops over medium–high heat until browned, about 2 minutes per side. Drain any accumulated liquid from pan. Turn heat down to medium–low and add soup, water, *Yoshida's®* and garlic powder. Cook pork chops, uncovered, until cooked through, about 10–15 minutes.

❧ In a separate dish, toss cooked broccoli with rice.

❧ To serve, place pork chops on top of broccoli and rice mixture and garnish with sesame seeds and pepper.

Janice Stein San Rafael, CA

Hawaiian Style Pizza

serves eight

1 pre–made pizza crust *(such as Boboli)*
1/2 cup *Yoshida's® Hawaiian Sweet & Sour Sauce*
2 cups shredded Mozzarella cheese
1/2 pound Canadian bacon, sliced
1 green pepper, chopped
1 small can pineapple chunks, drained

❧ Preheat oven to 400° F.

❧ Place pizza crust on a pizza pan or stone and brush evenly with *Yoshida's®.* Layer on the cheese, Canadian bacon, green pepper and pineapple, respectively.

❧ Bake pizza for 20 minutes or until cheese is melted and pizza is very hot. Slice into wedges and serve immediately.

Pork

Sweet Baby Back Ribs

SWEET BABY BACK RIBS

serves four

2 pounds baby back ribs
1–1 1/2 cups *Yoshida's® Hawaiian Sweet & Sour Sauce*
3/4–1 cup *Yoshida's® Premium Steak Sauce*

❧ Preheat oven broiler.

❧ Combine both sauces in a small bowl. Place the ribs on a baking sheet and brush with some of the sauce before broiling.

❧ Broil ribs for about 45 minutes, basting with sauce every 10 minutes.

COUNTRY STYLE PORK RIBS

makes six to eight

1 cup *Yoshida's® Spicy Wing & Rib Sauce*
2 tablespoons brown sugar
1 teaspoon prepared spicy mustard
1 teaspoon salt
2 tablespoons cider vinegar
3 pounds lean country–style pork ribs
1 medium onion, sliced in rings

❧ In a medium–sized bowl mix the *Yoshida's,®* brown sugar, mustard, salt and vinegar. Set aside.

❧ Layer the ribs and onions into a crockpot and pour the sauce over them to cover. Cover the crockpot and cook on low heat for about 8 hours or until the ribs are very tender.

Hawaiian Style Sweet & Sour Kielbasa

HAWAIIAN STYLE SWEET & SOUR KIELBASA

serves four

2–3 cups pre–cooked Polska Kielbasa, cubed
1/2 cup chopped bell pepper
1/2 cup chopped onion
1 1/2 cups *Yoshida's*®*Hawaiian Sweet & Sour Sauce*
1 can pineapple chunks, drained
2 cups cooked white rice, warm
fresh rosemary and parsley *(optional garnish)*

❧ In heavy, large skillet, begin cooking Kielbasa over medium heat. When beginning to brown and heated through, drain excess liquid. Add bell pepper and onion to skillet and cook until just tender, about 5 minutes. Add *Yoshida's*® and pineapple and stir to coat. Turn heat to low and cover pan. Cook mixture about 5–10 more minutes to combine flavors.

❧ Divide rice onto four warmed plates. Serve Kielbasa over rice and garnish with fresh rosemary and parsley.

Connie Hart   Apple, CA

Pork

Peppers Stuffed with Beef & Cheddar

PEPPERS STUFFED WITH BEEF & CHEDDAR

serves four

4 large green bell peppers

Filling:
1 pound lean ground beef
1 medium onion, diced
1/4 cup *Yoshida's® Spicy Wing & Rib Sauce* or *Yoshida's® Hawaiian Sweet & Sour Sauce*
1/4 teaspoon ground pepper
1 cup shredded Cheddar cheese

Sauce:
1 can unsalted tomato sauce
1/2 cup *Yoshida's® Spicy Wing & Rib Sauce* or *Yoshida's® Hawaiian Sweet & Sour Sauce*

❧ Cook beef in a large skillet over medium heat until just browned, about 5 minutes. Drain liquid from pan and add the onions. Cook another 3 minutes then add *Yoshida's®* and pepper and continue cooking another 2 minutes until the mixture is heated through. Set aside.

❧ Prepare peppers by cutting off tops about 1" down from the stem and scoop out the seeds and core. Divide the filling among peppers and place some cheese over the filling. Replace each pepper top and place peppers into a baking pan just large enough to fit peppers snugly.

❧ Preheat oven to 350° F. In a small saucepan mix together tomato sauce and *Yoshida's®* and heat the sauce until bubbly. Pour over and around peppers and cover the pan. Place the pan on middle shelf of oven and bake for 1 hour or until peppers are tender and the filling is heated through. Serve hot.

Cheese Steak Sandwich

73

Cheese Steak Sandwich

serves five

3/4 cup *Yoshida's*® *Premium Steak Sauce*
16 ounces beef tenderloin, cut in 1/2" strips
1/2 red bell pepper, julienne sliced
1/2 yellow bell pepper, julienne sliced
1/2 green bell pepper, julienne sliced
1/2 sweet onion, sliced or chopped
5 slices Provolone cheese, cut in halves
5 French rolls

❧ Marinate beef in 1/2 cup *Yoshida's*® for a minimum of 1 hour.

❧ When ready to assemble, cook drained meat in a medium–sized skillet over medium–high heat until just beginning to brown, about 2 minutes.

❧ Add vegetables to the skillet and sautè until softened and meat is cooked through, about 3 more minutes. Add remaining *Yoshida's*® to pan and cook 1 minute.

❧ Toast rolls, divide the meat mixture onto one half of each roll and place 2 slices of cheese over mixture. Serve hot, either open–faced or closed.

Beef Stroganoff

serves four

3 tablespoons butter or margarine
1 1/2 pounds round steak, cut into strips
2 cups halved mushrooms
1 medium onion, diced
2 tablespoons all–purpose flour
1 cup sour cream
3 ounces softened cream cheese
1/4 cup *Yoshida's*® *Original Gourmet Sauce*
8 ounce package egg noodles, cooked

❧ In a medium–sized skillet cook meat in butter over medium–high heat until lightly browned on all sides, about 3–5 minutes. Add mushrooms and onions. Continue cooking until meat is cooked through and vegetables are just beginning to brown, about 3–5 more minutes.

❧ Sprinkle flour over mixture and stir to coat well.

❧ Blend together sour cream, cream cheese and *Yoshida's*.® Stir into meat mixture. Reduce heat to medium and cook until sauce thickens, about 5 minutes.

❧ Serve over noodles.

STUFFED CABBAGE ROLLS

serves four

1 medium to large green cabbage
1 pound lean ground beef, browned
2 cups cooked white rice
1 small onion, finely chopped
1 cup dried bread crumbs
2 eggs
pinch ground pepper

pinch garlic powder
pinch onion salt
pinch salt
1/4 cup *Yoshida's® Traditional Teriyaki Sauce*
1 1/4 cup *Yoshida's® Hawaiian Sweet & Sour Sauce*
1 tablespoon lemon juice
1/2 teaspoon cinnamon

❧ Put a large pot of water on to boil. Keeping cabbage head intact, cut off as much of the stem as possible. Place cabbage in hot water and bring to a boil. Turn heat down to a slow simmer and cook 10–15 minutes, or until the outer leaves are easily removeable. Remove the first 12 outer leaves, making sure they are pliable enough to roll, and set aside to drain.

❧ Preheat oven to 375° F.

❧ In a large bowl, mix the beef, rice, onions, bread crumbs, eggs, seasonings and 1/4 cup each of *Yoshida's® Sauces*. Place 1/3 cup of filling near the base of each cabbage leaf. Roll up tightly, folding in the sides. Place the rolls seam–side down in a buttered or non–stick baking pan and set aside.

❧ In a small bowl, stir the remaining 1 cup *Yoshida's® Hawaiian Sweet & Sour Sauce* with the lemon juice and cinnamon. Spoon small amount over the cabbage rolls, cover pan.

❧ Bake on middle shelf of oven for 20–25 minutes. Serve hot with extra sauce.

Stuffed Cabbage Rolls

76

Italian-Style Meatloaf

serves four

1 pound lean ground beef
1 pound bulk Italian sausage
1 medium onion, diced
1 teaspoon minced fresh garlic
2 cups bread crumbs or crushed corn chips
1/4 cup *Yoshida's® Original Gourmet Sauce*
1/2 cup *Yoshida's® Hawaiian Sweet & Sour Sauce*

❧ This recipe can be cooked in the oven or the microwave. Preheat oven to 350° F if baking in oven. In a large bowl, mix together beef, sausage, onion and garlic. Add bread crumbs or corn chips and mix thoroughly. Stir in sauces.

❧ Shape mixture into a loaf pan. Place on middle rack of oven and bake for 1 hour or until cooked through.

❧ To bake in the microwave, form mixture in a circle around a small glass in a microwave safe dish. The glass will allow even cooking as well as absorb oil from meat. Cover and cook on high for about 15 minutes or until browned. Do not remove glass after cooking until oil has cooled and hardened.

Country Meatloaf & Vegetables

serves four

1 1/2 pounds ground beef
3/4 cup dry bread crumbs
1/4 cup diced onion
1/4 cup *Yoshida's® Premium Steak Sauce*
2 tablespoons *Yoshida's® Original Gourmet Sauce*
1/2 teaspoon ground pepper
2 eggs, beaten
6 medium potatoes, quartered
6 medium carrots, cut into 2" pieces

fresh rosemary sprigs *(optional)*
fresh mushrooms *(optional)*

❧ Preheat the oven to 375° F.

❧ In a large mixing bowl combine ground beef, bread crumbs and onion. Add sauces, pepper and eggs. Blend well.

❧ In a 3–quart baking dish, firmly shape the meatloaf into an 8"x 4" loaf. Surround the meat with potatoes and carrots. Place baking dish on middle shelf of oven and bake for 50–60 minutes or until cooked through.

❧ Let meatloaf cool for 10 minutes before slicing. Garnish with rosemary and fresh mushrooms if desired.

Country Meatloaf & Vegetables

Beef Pot Roast

serves eight

4–5 pounds beef chuck roast
1 clove fresh garlic, minced
3/4 cup sour cream
3 tablespoons flour
2 celery stalks, chopped
1 medium onion, quartered
2 carrots, chopped in large pieces
1/2 cup dry red wine
1/2 cup *Yoshida's® Traditional Teriyaki Sauce*
2 large red or white potatoes, cut in large pieces *(optional)*

❧ Rub roast with garlic and put in crockpot. In a small bowl, mix together the sour cream and flour. Add mixture to crockpot. Cover and cook on low heat for 6–7 hours.

❧ Add the celery, onion, carrots, wine and sauce to crockpot, mix well. Cover and cook for another hour or until the vegetables are tender. If adding potatoes, add to crockpot with other vegetables.

Beef Roast with Horseradish

serves four

2 pounds beef chuck roast
1 1/3 cup *Yoshida's® Original Gourmet Sauce*
4 ounces Horseradish sauce
1 teaspoon garlic salt
1 teaspoon ground pepper

❧ This recipe works well for cooking in the oven or the microwave.

❧ Place the beef in an oven or microwave proof baking dish. Pour 1 cup of *Yoshida's®* over the beef and marinate at room temperature for 1 hour. Mix the remaining sauce with Horseradish sauce and set aside.

❧ Preheat oven to 350° F.

❧ Season beef with salt and pepper and spread the Horseradish mixture over beef.

❧ Cover and place on middle rack of oven or in center of the microwave.

❧ Bake in oven for 1 hour or in microwave on high for 5 minutes, turning dish and then setting on defrost for another 15–20 minutes.

❧ If desired, add chopped carrots and potatoes to dish to make a complete meal.

Beef

Stir Fry Broccoli with Beef
serves four to six

1 1/2 pounds lean boneless round steak
1 cup dry white wine
3/4 cup *Yoshida's® Traditional Teriyaki Sauce*
6 tablespoons water
3 tablespoons honey
2 tablespoons cornstarch
2 tablespoons vegetable oil
5 cups broccoli florets
1 medium red pepper, sliced

❧ Trim fat from steak. Slice steak diagonally across the grain into 1/4" strips. Place meat in a zip–top heavy duty plastic bag. Combine 2/3 cup wine and 1/2 cup *Yoshida's®* and pour into bag. Shake bag to evenly coat steak and refrigerate for 2 hours or overnight.

❧ When ready to prepare dish, heat wok or skillet. Combine water, honey and cornstarch. Set aside.

❧ Add 1 tablespoon oil to wok and stir fry broccoli about 4 minutes. Remove broccoli from wok, set aside and keep warm. Next, remove steak from marinade. Add remaining oil and steak to wok and stir fry for 4 minutes or until done. Add red pepper and broccoli, toss. Stir in honey mixture, 1/3 cup wine, 1/4 cup *Yoshida's®* and cook until thoroughly heated and sauce begins to thicken. Serve over rice.

Traditional Yakiniku Beef
serves four

1 cup *Yoshida's® Yakiniku Sauce*
12 ounces beef tenderloin, cut into strips
toasted sesame seeds

❧ Marinate beef strips in *Yoshida's® Yakiniku Sauce* for a minimum of 30 minutes.

❧ On hot grill or skillet, flash cook beef strips to desired temperature. Serve with steamed white rice. Use additional sauce and sesame seeds for dipping.

Teriyaki Burgers

Teriyaki Burgers

serves four

1 pound lean ground beef
1/4 teaspoon pepper
1/2 cup *Yoshida's® Traditional Teriyaki Sauce*
4 slices Cheddar or Swiss cheese
4 pineapple rings
4 hamburger buns
lettuce and onion *(optional)*

❧ Prepare grill or heat broiler.

❧ In a medium–sized bowl, mix the ground beef, pepper and *Yoshida's®* thoroughly. Shape into patties and grill or broil to desired doneness. Place cheese on top of hamburger and top with pineapple. Serve on warm buns.

❧ You may also choose to grill or broil the pineapple at the same time, as this imparts a nice carmelized flavor.

Sloppy Joes

serves six

2 pounds lean ground beef
1 1/4 cups *Yoshida's® Hawaiian Sweet & Sour Sauce*
1/2 cup diced green peppers
1/4 teaspoon black pepper
6 hamburger buns

❧ In a medium–sized skillet, brown ground beef and drain any liquid left in the pan. Add *Yoshida's®,* bell peppers and black pepper. Mix well. Serve hot on warm toasted buns.

Beef

Savory Beef Pot Pie

SAVORY BEEF POT PIE

serves four

2 9" pie crusts *(defrosted if frozen)*
2 tablespoons butter
1 pound stew meat, cubed into 1" pieces
2 large carrots, chopped
2 celery stalks, chopped
1/2 medium onion, chopped
2 small zucchinis, chopped
1 can chicken gravy

1/2 teaspoon ground pepper
1 teaspoon sage
3/4 cup *Yoshida's® Hawaiian Sweet & Sour Sauce*
1/2 cup *Yoshida's® Original Gourmet Sauce*
1 tablespoon flour
1 tablespoon cornstarch
3 tablespoons water

❧ Preheat oven to 350˚ F.

❧ Line one 9" pie dish or 2 small casserole dishes with pie crust. Set aside.

❧ Melt 1 tablespoon butter in large skillet. Add stew meat and cook over medium–high heat until browned, approximately 3–5 minutes. Transfer meat to a plate and add the remaining tablespoon of butter. Turn heat down to medium and sautè carrots, celery and onions until tender, about 3 minutes. Add zucchini to the skillet and cook 30 seconds. Return beef to skillet along with gravy and seasonings. Stir well and add the *Yoshida's®* sauces. Bring the liquid to a boil, turn heat down to low and cook 5 minutes.

❧ Combine flour, cornstarch and water. Add to the pot pie mixture, stirring until the sauce thickens, about 5 more minutes. Spoon mixture into prepared crust, crimp top crust over pie and make 3 two inch vents in top crust. Set the pie pans on a baking sheet on middle shelf of oven and bake for 30 minutes.

Alice Volkens Jackson, NJ

Beef

"Korokei" Beef

serves four

1 small onion, chopped
2 medium Russet potatoes, peeled and cubed
1 pound lean ground beef
salt and pepper
1 cup flour
1–2 eggs, beaten
bread crumbs
oil
Any *Yoshida's® Fine Sauces*

❧ In a small pan, cover chopped onion with water and simmer until soft. Drain and set aside to cool.

❧ Boil potatoes for 10–15 minutes in same water as onions. Drain, place in large bowl and let cool. With a fork, partially mash potatoes. Mix in beef and onions and season with salt and pepper. Stir well to combine and form into 2"–3" patties.

❧ Place the flour on a large plate, the eggs in a medium–sized bowl and the bread crumbs on another plate. To assemble: coat patties with flour, dip in beaten egg and roll in bread crumbs. When all patties are assembled, fry in oil until golden, about 1–2 minutes per side and drain on paper towels.

❧ Transfer to a warm plate and drizzle with any of *Yoshida's® Fine Sauces.*

Mrs. Jim Fox Los Angeles, CA

Jerky

makes one pound

1 pound lean red meat *(venison or beef)*
1 cup *Yoshida's® Original Gourmet Sauce*
1 cup *Yoshida's® Traditional Teriyaki Sauce*
1 tablespoon Liquid Smoke
1 tablespoon cayenne pepper

❧ Slice the meat into 1/4" thick strips. Mix both sauces, Liquid Smoke and cayenne pepper together in a non–metal dish and marinate meat strips in refrigerator for 24 hours.

❧ Smoke the meat or dehydrate the meat slowly in the oven at 150° F. until desired consistency is reached.

Poultry

Mandarin Orange Chicken
serves four

4 boneless, skinless chicken breasts
1 11 ounce can Mandarin Orange segments
2 tablespoons rice vinegar
2 tablespoons mirin or sherry
1/2 cup Yoshida's® Original Gourmet Sauce
2 tablespoons canola oil
2 tablespoons Yoshida's® Original Gourmet Sauce
cooked white rice
parsley or cilantro (garnish)

❧ Combine chicken breasts, Mandarin Oranges and their juice, vinegar, mirin and 1/2 cup Yoshida's® Marinate for 2 hours in refrigerator.

❧ Heat a medium-sized skillet or wok on medium-high and add oil. Remove chicken from marinade and reserve marinade.

❧ Sautè chicken until lightly browned on each side, about 1 minute per side. Remove chicken onto a paper towel and blot off excess oil. Wipe skillet clean. Return chicken and marinade to skillet. Turn heat to medium and continue cooking until sauce is reduced and chicken is cooked through, about 3–5 minutes.

❧ Serve chicken over rice, drizzle with the remaining 2 tablespoons Yoshida's® and garnish with parsley or cilantro if desired.

Helen Rubin Palo Alto, CA

Sesame Chicken
serves two

2 boneless, skinless chicken breasts, cut in 1" cubes
1/4 cup Yoshida's® Quick & Easy Stir Fry Sauce
1 tablespoon cornstarch
1/4 cup chicken broth
2 tablespoons oil
3 celery stalks, sliced in 1/2" pieces
4 green onions, sliced in 1/2" pieces
1 cup steamed white rice
2 tablespoons sesame seeds

❧ Marinate chicken pieces in Yoshida's® for 30 minutes.

❧ Mix together cornstarch and chicken broth and set aside.

❧ Heat oil in a wok or skillet on medium-high and stir fry celery and onions for about 2 minutes until crisp and tender. Remove from pan. Add a little more oil to the pan if needed.

❧ Drain chicken and reserve marinade. Turn the heat down to medium and stir fry chicken for about 3 minutes. Add the reserved marinade to broth mixture and add to the pan, stirring well to blend. After mixture is thickened and chicken is thoroughly cooked, about 3 more minutes, add vegetables back to the pan and stir fry several more minutes.

❧ Serve over rice and sprinkle with sesame seeds.

86

Lemon & Garlic Cornish Game Hens

LEMON & GARLIC CORNISH GAME HENS

serves four

4 cornish game hens
1/2 cup *Yoshida's® Traditional Teriyaki Sauce*
1 tablespoon grated lemon peel
1 tablespoon fresh lemon juice
2 cloves fresh garlic, minced
1/4 teaspoon ground red pepper or chili flakes
1 tablespoon fresh minced cilantro
1 lemon, thinly sliced

❧ To prepare the hens: remove and discard giblets and neck. Split hens lengthwise by removing the backbone. Rinse them under cold water, drain and pat dry. Place the hens in a large ziplock bag or glass 9"x13" pan.

❧ To make marinade: combine *Yoshida's®*, lemon peel, lemon juice, garlic and red pepper. Pour over the hens and refrigerate 8 hours or overnight, turning hens occasionally.

❧ Prepare broiler or grill. Reserving marinade, remove hens and place on rack of broiler pan or grill. If broiling, place hens about 8" from heat source and cook 45–50 minutes or until tender, turning over frequently and basting with reserved marinade.

❧ Remove to serving platter and garnish with fresh cilantro and lemons.

MUSHROOM & CHEESE STUFFED CHICKEN

serves two to three

4 boneless, skinless chicken thighs
2 cups *Yoshida's® Original Gourmet Sauce*
1 cup sliced mushrooms
1 teaspoon sweet basil
4 slices Swiss cheese
8 toothpicks
garlic salt *(to taste)*
pepper *(to taste)*

❧ Marinate chicken thighs in *Yoshida's®* for 30 minutes, refrigerate.

❧ Preheat oven to 350° F. while preparing chicken.

❧ Mix mushrooms and basil together in small bowl. Drain thighs from marinade and lay on a baking sheet to assemble. Lay thighs flat and place a slice of cheese on each one. Top with 1/4 of mushroom mixture and roll up chicken lengthwise. Thread 2 toothpicks through each thigh to keep closed during baking. Sprinkle with garlic salt and pepper.

❧ Bake for 1–1 1/2 hours. Serve hot.

Poultry

Chicken Fajitas

Chicken Fajitas

makes eight

2 tablespoons oil
1 medium onion, julienne sliced
1 medium green pepper, julienne sliced
1 medium red pepper, julienne sliced
1 pound boneless, skinless chicken breasts *(about 3)*
3/4 cup *Yoshida's®Original Gourmet Sauce*
8 flour tortillas, warmed

❧ Heat oil in a wok or skillet until hot and sautè onion and bell peppers until just soft, about 2 minutes. Remove with a slotted spoon to a plate and set aside.

❧ Cut the chicken breasts into 1/2" strips and sautè in same pan for about 5 minutes or until no longer pink. Return vegetables to the pan along with the sauce and cook mixture until sauce comes to a boil and thickens. Remove pan from heat.

❧ Spoon the chicken and vegetable mixture into warmed tortillas, roll up and serve.

❧ *Salsa, sour cream and guacamole are nice accompaniments.*

Chicken Burritos

makes eight

6–8 boneless, skinless chicken breasts or thighs
1 tablespoon oil
1 cup *Yoshida's®Traditional Teriyaki Sauce*
2 green onions, chopped
1/2 cup chopped tomatoes
1/2 cup shredded lettuce
3/4 cup shredded Cheddar cheese
sour cream
8 10–inch flour tortillas

❧ Heat oil in a large skillet over medium–high heat and cook chicken until almost done (thighs will take longer to cook than breasts.) Drain all liquid from pan. Add *Yoshida's®*and bring to a boil. Continue cooking until the sauce reduces and thickens and chicken is fully cooked.

❧ Remove chicken, set aside and let cool slightly. Slice chicken into strips.

❧ Fill warm tortillas with chicken strips, green onion, tomato, lettuce, cheese and sour cream. Fold in the end of the tortilla and roll into a burrito.

Spicy Wine Poached Chicken

serves four

4 boneless, skinless chicken breasts or thighs
1/2 cup dry white wine
3/4 cup *Yoshida's® Spicy Wing & Rib Sauce*
1 tablespoon lemon juice
1/8 teaspoon salt

❧ Combine wine, *Yoshida's,®* lemon juice and salt in a skillet over medium–low heat. Bring the poaching liquid to just under a boil. Add chicken and reduce heat to low. Poach for 10–12 minutes or until chicken is cooked through.

❧ Serve with rice or noodles.

Chicken & Spinach Pie with Buttermilk Biscuits

serves eight

Filling:

2 cups cooked & shredded chicken
3/4 cup diced onion
10 ounces frozen spinach (*thawed & chopped*)
2 ounces diced pimento
1 cup lite sour cream
1 egg, beaten
1 cup *Yoshida's® Hawaiian Sweet & Sour Sauce*
1/2 teaspoon salt
1/2 teaspoon ground pepper

pinch of nutmeg
2 cloves fresh garlic, minced

Biscuits:

2/3 cup flour
2 teaspoons baking powder
1/2 teaspoon salt
3/4 cup buttermilk
1/4 cup melted butter

❧ Preheat oven to 375° F.

❧ In a large bowl, combine chicken, onion, spinach and pimento. In a small bowl, stir together sour cream, egg, *Yoshida's®* and seasonings. Add to the chicken mixture.

❧ Spread the filling evenly into a 9" greased pie plate and set aside.

❧ Make biscuits by stirring dry ingredients together in a medium–sized bowl. Add buttermilk and melted butter and stir gently to combine. Do not overmix. Drop dough by a large tablespoon onto filling.

❧ Bake for 45 minutes or until filling is heated through and biscuits are golden brown.

Gourmet BBQ Chicken

serves four

1 1/2 pounds boneless, skinless chicken breasts or thighs
1 cup *Yoshida's®Original Gourmet Sauce*
1 teaspoon olive oil
2 tablespoons sugar
1 cup pineapple juice
1 teaspoon crushed red pepper
1 cup 7–Up or Sprite
1/2 cup chopped scallions
salt *(to taste)*

❧ To prepare chicken, cut into 3"x3" cubes and rinse in a strainer. Let dry a few minutes.

❧ To prepare the marinade, mix all ingredients together in a large bowl. Place the chicken in a large zip lock bag and add the marinade. Seal tightly and keep refrigerated at least 8 hours or up to 24 hours.

❧ Prepare grill and barbecue chicken pieces about 10–15 minutes or until juices run clear.

Ray Balingit   North Plainfield, NJ

Demo Chicken

makes twelve to sixteen

1 1/2–2 pounds chicken wingettes, drumettes or boneless, skinless thighs
3/4 cup *Yoshida's®Original Gourmet Sauce*

❧ Heat a large skillet on medium heat and add the chicken. Cover and cook 15–20 minutes. Turn chicken several times until cooked through.

❧ Drain all liquid from the pan and lower heat to medium–low. Add the *Yoshida's®* and stir to coat evenly. Return temperature to medium and replace lid.

❧ Cook for 10 more minutes, turning chicken a few times to coat evenly.

❧ Remove lid and continue cooking another 5 minutes to reduce sauce to a glaze.

❧ Serve immediately.

Poultry

Poultry

GRILLED CHICKEN & VEGETABLES

serves four to six

1 1/2 pounds boneless, skinless chicken breasts
2 sweet potatoes, sliced
1 cup *Yoshida's® Original Gourmet Sauce*
1 cup sliced red peppers
2 white potatoes, sliced
1 medium summer squash, sliced
1 onion, cubed
1 cup mushrooms
1 medium zucchini, sliced

❧ Marinate chicken in *Yoshida's®* for several hours. When ready to barbecue, prepare grill and remove chicken from the marinade, reserving it. Cook chicken until almost done, basting with marinade on each side during cooking. Set aside and keep warm.

❧ In a grill basket, start cooking the vegetables according to length of time they will take to cook. Start with sweet potatoes and allow them to cook 3/4 of the way to being done. Add remaining vegetables and cook until tender. Just before they are done, return the chicken to the grill and baste once again. Cook until done.

❧ Slice chicken breasts and toss together with the other vegetables. Serve warm.

M.A. McGroarty   Ocala, FL

CASHEW CHICKEN

serves four

1 pound boneless, skinless chicken breasts
1/2 cup *Yoshida's® Original Gourmet Sauce*
3 tablespoons oil
1/2 onion, cut in 1/4" slices
1 cup mixed peas and carrots
1/2 cup snow peas
3 green onions *(scallions)*
1 red pepper, cut in 1/4" slices
1 teaspoon cornstarch
1/2 cup water
1/2 cup whole cashew nuts

❧ Cut chicken into 1/4" slices, place in bowl and add *Yoshida's®.* Marinate chicken 15 minutes.

❧ In a wok or skillet heat the oil on high and add the onions. Sautè for 30 seconds, add chicken with the marinade and stir fry for 2–3 minutes. Add the carrots, peas, snow peas, green onions and red peppers. Stir fry another 2–3 minutes.

❧ Combine cornstarch with water and add to the pan. Mix well for another minute to thicken sauce.

❧ Add cashews and toss lightly. Serve over rice or noodles.

Cashew Chicken

94

Poultry

Roast Gourmet Turkey Breast

serves four

1 cup *Yoshida's® Original Gourmet Sauce*
1 cup *Yoshida's® Special Blend Deli Sauce*
1 1/2–2 pounds bone–in turkey breast
1 cup chicken stock
2 cloves fresh garlic, minced
1/2 teaspoon salt
1 teaspoon ground pepper
1 cup pearl onions
1/2 pound new potatoes
1 cup baby carrots

❧ Mix *Yoshida's®* sauces together and pour over turkey breast. Marinate overnight.

❧ Preheat the oven to 350° F. Let turkey sit at room temperature while oven preheats.

❧ In a shallow roasting pan, place turkey, marinade, chicken stock, garlic, salt and pepper. Place in the lower third of the oven. Bake for 35 minutes, basting every 10 minutes. Remove from the oven and add the onions, potatoes and carrots to the roasting pan. Coat all vegetables in the liquid and return the pan to the oven. Bake for another 30–40 minutes or until turkey is cooked through and vegetables are tender.

❧ Let turkey rest for 30 minutes out of the oven before slicing. Serve turkey with the vegetables and the pan juices.

Hawaiian Sweet & Sour Turkey

serves four

1/4 cup sake
1 3/4 cup *Yoshida's® Hawaiian Sweet & Sour Sauce*
1 pound boneless, skinless turkey breasts
1 cup sliced Japanese eggplant
2 cups sliced mushrooms
1/2 medium red onion, cut in wedges
1 clove fresh garlic, minced
1 teaspoon ginger root powder
1 teaspoon crushed red pepper flakes

❧ In a small bowl blend sake with *Yoshida's®*. In a large zip–lock bag or shallow dish, marinate turkey in 3/4 cup of the sauce blend. Refrigerate for 1 hour.

❧ Prepare the grill or preheat broiler. Remove turkey from marinade, discard marinade. Grill or broil turkey until done, basting with 2/3 cup of sauce blend. Set aside to cool.

❧ Heat a large non–stick skillet over medium–high heat and sauté eggplant for 3 minutes. Add the mushrooms and cook another 3 minutes. Add onion, garlic and ginger and sautè another 3 minutes. Pour in the remaining 1/3 cup sauce blend with red pepper flakes. Make a ring of vegetables on platter and fan turkey breast over vegetables. Garnish with red peppers.

95

Hawaiian Sweet & Sour Turkey

Teriyaki Chicken Sandwich

Teriyaki Chicken Sandwich

makes four

4 boneless, skinless chicken breasts or thighs
1 cup *Yoshida's® Traditional Teriyaki Sauce*
1/2 cup diced sweet peppers
1-1/2 cups crushed pineapple
2 cups *Yoshida's® Hawaiian Sweet & Sour Sauce*
4 slices ham or Canadian bacon
4 slices Swiss cheese
4 hamburger buns

❧ Marinate chicken in 1/2 cup *Yoshida's® Traditional Teriyaki Sauce* for 1 hour. Grill or broil chicken, basting with remaining 1/2 cup sauce, till just done and set aside.

❧ In a small saucepan heat peppers and pineapple with *Yoshida's® Hawaiian Sweet & Sour Sauce* until hot.

❧ To assemble sandwich: On each bun, place a chicken breast, ham slice, cheese and pineapple mixture. Serve hot.

Creamy Chicken Stuffed Pitas

makes twelve

1 pound boneless, skinless chicken thighs
2 cups *Yoshida's® Original Gourmet Sauce*
1 medium head of lettuce, shredded
1 large tomato, diced
1 cucumber, diced
1 cup shredded Cheddar cheese
3/4 cup ranch dressing
6 pita pocket breads, cut in half

❧ Marinate chicken in *Yoshida's®* for about 30 minutes. Grill or broil until done and cut into 1" cubes. Set aside.

❧ In a large bowl, toss together lettuce, tomato, cucumber and cheese. Add cut up chicken to the bowl and drizzle dressing over the mixture. Toss well to combine all ingredients.

❧ Stuff each pita half with mixture and serve.

Poultry

Poultry

Sweet & Sour Chicken

serves four

Shirley Temple Chicken Wings

makes twenty-four to thirty-two

1 cup packaged rice pilaf blend

2 cups chicken broth

1/2 teaspoon garlic salt

salt & ground pepper *(to taste)*

1 pound boneless, skinless chicken breasts

1 tablespoon oil

1 green onion, thinly sliced

1/2 red bell pepper, diced

1/2 green bell pepper, diced

1 cup *Yoshida's® Hawaiian Sweet & Sour Sauce*

4 pounds chicken wings

1 green bell pepper, sliced

1 red bell pepper, sliced

3 cups *Yoshida's® Hawaiian Sweet & Sour Sauce*

2 tablespoons grenadine

2 tablespoons apple cider vinegar

16 ounces pineapple chunks *(reserve juice)*

6 ounces cherries in juice, drained

1 teaspoon sugar

1 tablespoon cornstarch

❧ Cook rice pilaf in the broth with both salts and pepper until tender, about 20 minutes. Remove from heat and set aside, covered.

❧ Cut chicken into bite–size pieces and sautè in oil, over medium–high heat for 30 seconds. Add green onions and peppers and continue cooking until chicken is cooked through and peppers are just softening, about 2 minutes. Add *Yoshida's,®* turn heat to low and simmer until sauce is hot.

❧ Serve Sweet and Sour Chicken over rice.

❧ Preheat oven to 375° F. Arrange chicken on a baking sheet and place on middle rack of oven. Bake wings for 45 minutes, drain and coat with 2 cups *Yoshida's.®* Return wings to oven and cook another 10 minutes.

❧ In a non–stick skillet, sautè bell peppers over medium heat until just softened, about 3 minutes. Pour in remaining 1 cup *Yoshida's®* and heat to a boil. Turn heat down to low and add grenadine, vinegar and pineapple. Stir well and add the cherries.

❧ In a small bowl, stir together pineapple juice, sugar and cornstarch. Add to the skillet and stir until heated through and thickened.

❧ When wings are done, remove from oven and arrange on a platter. Cover with sauce and serve.

Loetta White   Alma, AR

Mike Canik   Hayward, WI

CHICKEN CALZONES

m a k e s   s i x

Crust:

1 package active dry yeast

1 cup warm water

1 tablespoon sugar

2 teaspoons vegetable oil

1/2 teaspoon salt

1 1/2 cups flour

1/4 cup whole wheat flour

1 egg white, beaten

Filling:

1 cup cooked and shredded chicken

1 cup chopped mushrooms

1 cup shredded Mozzarella cheese

1/4 cup chopped onion

1/3 cup *Yoshida's*®*Hawaiian Sweet & Sour Sauce*

2 tablespoons grated Parmesan cheese

❧ Prepare crust by dissolving yeast in a large bowl with warm water. Stir in sugar, oil, salt and flours to make a smooth dough. Turn out onto floured surface and knead until smooth, about 5 minutes. Place dough back in bowl. Cover and let rest 5 minutes.

❧ Preheat oven to 375°F.

❧ Prepare filling by combining chicken, mushrooms, Mozzarella and onion in a large bowl. Drizzle on the *Yoshida's*® and mix gently.

❧ Spray baking sheet with non–stick cooking spray. Divide dough into 6 equal parts. On floured surface, roll each part into a 7" circle and place 1/3 cup of filling on one half of dough. Fold dough over filling and press the edges together with a fork to seal. Place calzones on baking sheet and brush surface with egg white. Cut several slits in top of surface and sprinkle Parmesan over the tops.

❧ Bake for 25–30 minutes. Serve hot

Poultry

Poultry

LEMON & GINGER CHICKEN WITH PINEAPPLE

serves four

4 boneless, skinless chicken breasts

3/4 cup *Yoshida's® Original Gourmet Sauce*

2 tablespoons lemon juice

2 teaspoons sesame oil

1 teaspoon minced fresh garlic

1 small onion, thinly sliced

2 teaspoons fresh grated ginger

1 lemon, thinly sliced

4 cups steamed rice

1 cup sliced water chestnuts, drained

1/2 cup diced carrots

1 cup baby peas, cooked

3 green onions, thinly sliced

1 teaspoon fresh tarragon

1/4 cup sliced toasted almonds

1 1/2 cups pineapple chunks

❧ Place chicken breasts in a small baking dish and pour 1/2 cup of *Yoshida's®* and lemon juice over the chicken, turning to coat. Refrigerate for 1 hour.

❧ Add 1 teaspoon sesame oil to a heated, medium–sized skillet or wok and sautè garlic, onions and ginger over medium heat for 2–3 minutes or until soft and beginning to brown. Remove mixture with a slotted spoon to a small bowl and set aside.

❧ To the same skillet, add remaining oil and drained chicken breasts, reserving marinade. Cook each side until lightly browned, about 2 minutes per side. Pour reserved marinade over chicken and turn heat down to medium–low. Sprinkle onion mixture over the chicken and arrange lemon slices on top. Cover the skillet and simmer until done.

❧ Mix the rice, water chestnuts, carrots and peas together in a bowl and portion onto plates.

❧ Place a chicken breast on each mound of rice mixture and garnish with the green onions, tarragon, almonds and pineapple. Drizzle remaining 1/4 cup of *Yoshida's®* over chicken. Serve immediately.

Teresa Sendra–Anagnost   Van Nuys, CA

101

Lightly Smoked & Grilled Salmon

serves six

Apple, Alder, or Hickory wood chips
1 whole salmon filleted
Yoshida's® Original Gourmet Sauce
salt and pepper *(to taste)*

❧ Place one or two handfuls of your favorite wood chips in water to soak for at least an hour.

❧ Baste the salmon with *Yoshida's®* and refrigerate at least 1 hour.

❧ Prepare the grill by turning flame to low if using a gas grill or placing rack on highest position if using charcoal. Place a handful of chips on the lava rock or briquettes. Return rack to grilling position and prepare salmon.

❧ Remove salmon from refrigerator and brush on additional sauce. Season with pepper and salt. Place salmon on oiled grill, flesh side down, and close the lid. Cook the salmon about 15 minutes per side, brushing on more sauce after turning over. Serve immediately.

John Stratton Tacoma, WA

Fish Fillets with Pineapple Sauce

serves four

1 small can of pineapple chunks
1 clove fresh garlic, minced
1/4 teaspoon ground ginger
1 tablespoon minced green onions
5 tablespoons *Yoshida's® Traditional Teriyaki Sauce*
1 teaspoon white vinegar
1 pound sole fillets
2 teaspoons cornstarch
1 teaspoon sesame oil

❧ Make the marinade by combining 2 tablespoons juice from pineapple can, garlic, ginger, green onion, 3 tablespoons *Yoshida's®* and vinegar. Stir together well.

❧ Place fish fillets in a shallow dish and top with marinade. Refrigerate for 10 minutes. Preheat broiler.

❧ Place marinated fillets onto a greased broiler rack. Reserve marinade. Broil 5–6 minutes, basting with marinade, until just cooked through.

❧ To make sauce, stir together undrained pineapple, cornstarch and sesame oil in a small saucepan. Heat to a boil and cook a few minutes to thicken. Serve sauce with the fish.

BROILED HALIBUT

serves two

1/4 cup *Yoshida's® Original Gourmet Sauce*
2 6 ounce halibut steaks
lemon wedges

❧ Marinate halibut in *Yoshida's®* about 1 hour in the refrigerator, turning after 30 minutes.

❧ Broil 4 inches from heat source, allowing 10 minutes cooking time per inch of thickness or until halibut flakes easily when tested with a fork.

❧ Garnish with lemon wedges.

SEARED AHI TUNA STEAKS

serves four to six

4–6 Ahi tuna steaks
1 1/4 cup *Yoshida's® Original Gourmet Sauce*
1 cup rice vinegar
1 teaspoon ginger root powder
1/4 cup chopped fresh cilantro
sugar *(to taste)*
sesame seeds *(optional)*

1 pound fresh salad greens
crispy chow mein noodles
wasabi *(fresh cut if possible)*
pickled ginger

❧ Marinate tuna in 1/2 cup of *Yoshida's®* for 15–20 minutes. Discard marinade.

❧ Make dressing by combining the rice vinegar, ginger and cilantro. Balance the tartness with sugar to taste. Set aside.

❧ In a hot sautè pan heat remaining sauce until it begins to bubble and reduces to a glaze. Cook tuna steaks in sauce briefly until desired doneness is reached. Searing the outside of the fish and retaining a rare inside is recommended. Coat the fish with toasted sesame seeds if desired. Set aside.

❧ Dress the greens with dressing and divide onto plates. Sprinkle noodles on and around the greens. Cut the tuna diagonally in half and offset on top of the greens. Put a small amount of wasabi at one end of a slice of pickled ginger and roll the ginger into a cone shape.

❧ Place cone at the base of the tuna. Serve immediately.

Seared Ahi Tuna Steaks

Glazed Seafood Medley in Puff Pastry

Glazed Seafood Medley in Puff Pastry

serves four

4 puff pastry shells or 3" squares puff pastry *(grocers freezer, pastry)*
1/4 pound peeled rock shrimp
1/4 pound baby scallops
1/2 pound halibut, 1" chunks
3/4 cup *Yoshida's® Original Gourmet Sauce*
1/4 pound pearl onions
2 cups *Yoshida's® Classic Red Sweet & Sour Sauce*
1/4 cup chopped green onions

🌿 Bake the puff pastry according to package directions. If using squares, you can slice them in half from the side, once they are cooked, to create a top and bottom piece.

🌿 In a sautè pan gently cook the seafood. Using a slotted spoon, set seafood aside into a bowl, cover. Drain off any liquid left in the pan and pour in *Yoshida's® Original Gourmet Sauce*. Reduce the sauce to a glaze by simmering gently over medium heat for about 5 minutes. Add the onions and cook about 3 minutes. Next, return the seafood and any juices to the pan and cook just long enough to heat through.

🌿 To assemble: Swirl a generous amount of *Yoshida's® Classic Red Sweet & Sour Sauce* onto plates. Set the pastry shell in the center of plate and spoon glazed seafood into the shell. Top with pastry top as an option and sprinkle the green onions over all. You may wish to drizzle more glaze over dish. Serve immediately.

Shrimp Kabobs

makes six

1 pound shrimp, peeled and deveined *(21–25 per pound)*
1 1/2 large green peppers, cut into 1" pieces
1 1/2 large yellow peppers, cut into 1" pieces
1 large red pepper, cut into 1" pieces
1 medium sweet onion, cut into 1" pieces
1/2 cup *Yoshida's® Quick & Easy Stir Fry Sauce*
6 skewers

🌿 Combine cleaned shrimp with the cut vegetables in a shallow bowl and toss lightly with sauce. Refrigerate mixture at least one hour, turning the shrimp occasionally.

🌿 Prepare grill or broiler at least 15 minutes before cooking the kabobs. If using wooden skewers, soak them in water at least one hour before using.

🌿 Skewer kabobs by alternating shrimp and vegetables. Plan on using about 3–4 shrimp per skewer. Reserve the marinade.

🌿 Grill or broil the kabobs, basting with the reserved marinade, for several minutes on each side. Serve immediately.

Seafood

Teriyaki Fish Kabobs

TERIYAKI FISH KABOBS

makes eight

3/4 pound halibut, boned, cut in 1 1/2" chunks
3/4 pound salmon, boned, cut in 1 1/2" chunks
1 red pepper, cut into 1" pieces
1 yellow pepper, cut into 1" pieces
1/2 pound pearl onions
1/2 pound whole mushrooms
8 green onion tops
1 1/4 cup *Yoshida's® Traditional Teriyaki Sauce*
2 cups *Yoshida's® Classic Red Sweet & Sour Sauce*
1/4 cup chopped, fresh parsley
skewers

❧ Skewer the kabobs by alternating fish and vegetables. Place the kabobs in a shallow pan. Coat skewers with 3/4 cup *Yoshida's® Traditional Teriyaki Sauce*. Turn to cover all sides. Marinate kabobs in the refrigerator for at least 1 hour.

❧ Grill kabobs for 8–10 minutes, turning every few minutes and basting with remaining 1/2 cup *Yoshida's®*, until fish is cooked and vegetables are tender.

❧ Paint plates generously with *Yoshida's® Classic Red Sweet & Sour Sauce*. Place cooked kabobs on sauce and garnish with fresh parsley and serve immediately.

CRAB CHEESE DELIGHT

serves four

1 loaf French bread
2 cups real or imitation crab meat
1 cup shredded Cheddar or Swiss cheese
2 tablespoons *Yoshida's® Original Gourmet Sauce*

❧ Preheat the oven broiler.

❧ Split the French loaf in half lengthwise. Spread equal amounts of crab on each half and top with the cheese. Drizzle sauce over each half and place on a baking sheet. Place under broiler and cook until cheese is melted and bubbly.

❧ Let cool a few minutes and slice. Serve immediately.

Seafood

SWEET & SOUR SHRIMP STIR FRY

serves four

3 tablespoons oil
1/2 cup chopped green onions
1 5 ounce can water chestnuts, drained
1 5 ounce can bamboo shoots, drained
1 green bell pepper, julienne sliced
1 red bell pepper, julienne sliced
1 pound large shrimp, peeled and deveined
1/2 cup *Yoshida's® Hawaiian Sweet & Sour Sauce*
1 cup bean sprouts
4 cups cooked white rice

❧ Heat the oil in a wok or large skillet over medium–high heat and stir fry the green onions, water chestnuts and bamboo shoots about 1 minute. Add the bell peppers and shrimp and sauté another 2 minutes until shrimp is cooked. Pour in the *Yoshida's®* and toss to blend. Add the bean sprouts and toss once again.

❧ Serve immediately over steaming rice.

VEGETABLE STRUDEL

serves six to eight

1 cup sliced zucchini
1 cup broccoli florets
1 cup sliced mushrooms
1/4 cup diced red onion
3/4 cup *Yoshida's® Quick & Easy Stir Fry Sauce*
2 cups grated Swiss cheese

1 cup large bread crumbs or croutons
10 filo or strudel sheets *(grocers freezer section)*
1/2 cup melted butter or virgin olive oil
1 cup *Yoshida's® Hawaiian Sweet & Sour Sauce*
parsley or cilantro, chopped

❧ In a large skillet, sautè zucchini, broccoli, mushrooms and red onion over medium heat for 1 minute. Add *Yoshida's® Quick & Easy Stir Fry Sauce* and sautè another minute until vegetables just start to soften. Remove from heat. Let cool 5 minutes.

❧ In a large bowl toss together Swiss cheese and bread crumbs. Add vegetables to the bowl and mix together lightly. Chill 15–20 minutes.

❧ Preheat oven 375° F.

❧ Place 10 sheets of filo on a work surface and cover with a damp cloth. Brush each layer of dough with melted butter or oil until all sheets are stacked. (You may wish to make two smaller strudels by stacking 5 sheets per strudel and splitting filling evenly between the two.) Carefully spread filling down one long edge of filo sheet and roll up lengthwise. Make sure to brush oil or butter on the opposite edge to help seal the pastry.

❧ Bake strudel for 30 minutes or until golden brown and heated through. Remove from oven and set aside for 5–10 minutes before slicing. Heat *Yoshida's® Hawaiian Sweet & Sour Sauce* and pour a small amount on each plate. Serve a slice or two of strudel on each plate and sprinkle with parsley.

Savory Vegetable Pizza

Savory Vegetable Pizza

serves four to six

1 12" prepared pizza crust *(such as Boboli)*
1 envelope vegetable soup mix *(use only 1/2 of envelope)*
1 cup *Yoshida's® Hawaiian Sweet & Sour Sauce*
3 tablespoons olive oil
2 teaspoons basil leaves
1 clove garlic, minced
1/4 teaspoon ground pepper
2 cups shredded Mozzarella cheese
1 cup fresh sliced mushrooms
1 medium tomato, coarsley chopped
fresh basil leaves *(optional)*

❧ Preheat oven to 425° F.

❧ Set the pizza crust on a pizza pan or cookie sheet and set aside.

❧ In a small bowl combine soup mix, *Yoshida's®,* oil, basil, garlic and pepper. Spread mixture evenly over pizza shell. Sprinkle cheese evenly over sauce mixture and arrange mushrooms over the cheese. Sprinkle tomato pieces on last.

❧ Place pizza in oven and bake 20 minutes or until cheese is melted and crust is golden brown.

❧ Garnish with fresh basil leaves if desired.

Versatile Vegetable Delight

serves four

12 ounces cherry tomatoes
1/2 pound whole mushrooms
2 medium green bell peppers, cut into 1" squares
1 large red bell pepper, cut into 1" squares
1 medium red onion, cut into 1" squares
1/2 pound baby carrots–cleaned, blanched and cooled

Dressing:

2/3 cup light vegetable oil
3 tablespoons red wine vinegar
1 tablespoon dried parsley
1 tablespoon dried sweet basil
1 1/2 teaspoons garlic salt
1 teaspoon black pepper
dash of soy sauce
1 1/3 cups *Yoshida's®Hawaiian Sweet & Sour Sauce*

❧ Place all vegetables in a bowl. Prepare dressing by blending all ingredients together in a blender or by hand. Pour over vegetables and marinate for a minimum of 1 hour.

❧ This salad is great served alone or grilled on skewers and added to pasta.

VEGETABLE SHISH-KABOBS

serves four

2 green bell peppers, cut into 1" pieces
1 purple onion, cut into 1" pieces
2 boiled corn cobs, cut into 1" pieces
8 cherry tomatoes
8 large Crimini mushrooms, cut in half
2 cups *Yoshida's® Original Gourmet Sauce*
8 skewers

❧ Prepare the grill. Thread all vegetables onto skewers in alternating order.   In a small saucepan, slowly bring sauce to a boil. Lower heat and simmer until the sauce thickens and reduces to a glaze.

❧ Grill the skewers until tender, about 10 minutes, basting with sauce every few minutes.

Vegetarian

Vegetable Shish–Kabobs

Roast Lamb Chops with Apricots & Honey

Roast Lamb Chops with Apricots & Honey

serves two

6 dried apricots, diced
1 cup water
4 double loin lamb chops, 2" thick
1/4 cup olive oil
1/4 cup honey
1/4 cup *Yoshida's® Original Gourmet Sauce*
2 tablespoons Dijon mustard
1 teaspoon rosemary
1/2 teaspoon ground ginger

❧ Place apricots and water in a small saucepan. Heat to a simmer then remove. Let apricots sit in water 5 minutes. Drain, reserving water and set aside to cool.

❧ Prepare lamb chops by making a 1" deep by 1" wide pocket in the meaty side of each chop.

❧ Stuff apricots into pockets of lamb chops. Place chops in a shallow baking pan and set aside.

❧ Make the marinade by whisking the reserved apricot water with remaining ingredients in a small bowl. Pour marinade over lamb chops, cover and refrigerate, turning occasionally, for at least 2 hours.

❧ Preheat oven to 425° F. Bake lamb chops in marinade for 30–40 minutes or until lamb reaches desired doneness.

Veal Stroganoff

serves six

2 pounds veal for stew, cut in 1/2" pieces
2 tablespoons flour
1 1/4 cup baby carrots
1 cup pearl onions
2 cans Cream of Mushroom soup
1/2 cup *Yoshida's® Original Gourmet Sauce*
1/2 teaspoon thyme
2 teaspoons lemon juice
1 pound cooked egg noodles
1/2 cup sour cream

❧ In a large bowl, coat veal with flour and heat a large non–stick skillet over medium–high heat. Cook veal in batches until lightly browned. Set aside.

❧ In a steamer or saucepan, cook the carrots and onions until just tender. Set aside.

❧ In a 2 quart saucepan combine soup and *Yoshida's®* over medium heat. Add veal, carrots, onions, thyme and lemon juice. Heat thoroughly, about 5 minutes and serve on a bed of buttered noodles. Garnish with sour cream.

Specialty

Roast Lamb with Garlic, Rosemary & Lemon

serves four to six

1 4–5 pound leg of lamb, boned
6 large cloves fresh garlic, sliced into slivers
3 fresh rosemary sprigs
1 1/2 cups *Yoshida's® Original Gourmet Sauce*
1 cup fresh lemon juice
3 fresh rosemary sprigs, stems removed, needles chopped
2 tablespoons ground pepper
2 tablespoons rock salt
1 tablespoon onion powder
2 cups sliced mushrooms
1 medium white onion, quartered

❧ Preheat oven to 350° F.

❧ Make 1" deep cuts all over the leg of lamb and place garlic slivers into most of them. Break the rosemary sprigs into smaller pieces and stuff into the remaining cuts. Set aside.

❧ In a small bowl, mix together *Yoshida's®* and lemon juice. Pour 1 1/2 cups of sauce over lamb and rub all over to coat.

❧ In a small bowl, mix together remaining rosemary, pepper, rock salt and onion powder. Pour remaining sauce into a shallow roasting pan and cover with mushrooms and onions. Place the leg of lamb over vegetables and sprinkle evenly with the dry spice mixture.

❧ Place roasting pan in lower third of oven and bake lamb for 1 1/2 hours, or 18 minutes per pound for medium rare. Baste occasionally with pan juices.

❧ Let the roast stand for 20 minutes before carving. Serve lamb with pan juices.

Venison with Sour Cream & Mushrooms

serves six to eight

2 1/2 pounds *venison tenderloin, cut in 1/2" slices
3/4 teaspoon marjoram
1 teaspoon ground pepper
1/4 cup flour
2 tablespoons butter
2 medium onions, thinly sliced
1/2 pound fresh mushrooms, thinly sliced
1/4 cup dry sherry
1/3 cup *Yoshida's* ®*Original Gourmet Sauce*
1 beef bouillon cube
1/2 cup hot water
1/2 cup sour cream
2 tablespoons flour

Specialty

❧ Season the meat with the marjoram and pepper. Sprinkle the flour over the meat and toss to coat. Heat a large skillet over medium–high heat. Add the butter and sautè meat in batches until lightly browned, about 1 minute per side. Remove meat to a plate and reserve.

❧ Turn heat down to medium and sautè onions and mushrooms until just beginning to brown, about 3 minutes. Add the sherry and *Yoshida's.* ® Stir to mix. Dissolve the bouillon in the water and add to the skillet. Return the meat to the sauce and continue cooking until the meat is cooked to desired temperature.

❧ Combine the sour cream with the flour and stir into the skillet. Stir over medium–low heat until sauce thickens, about 5–10 minutes.

❧ **You may wish to substitute Buffalo, Elk or Beef*

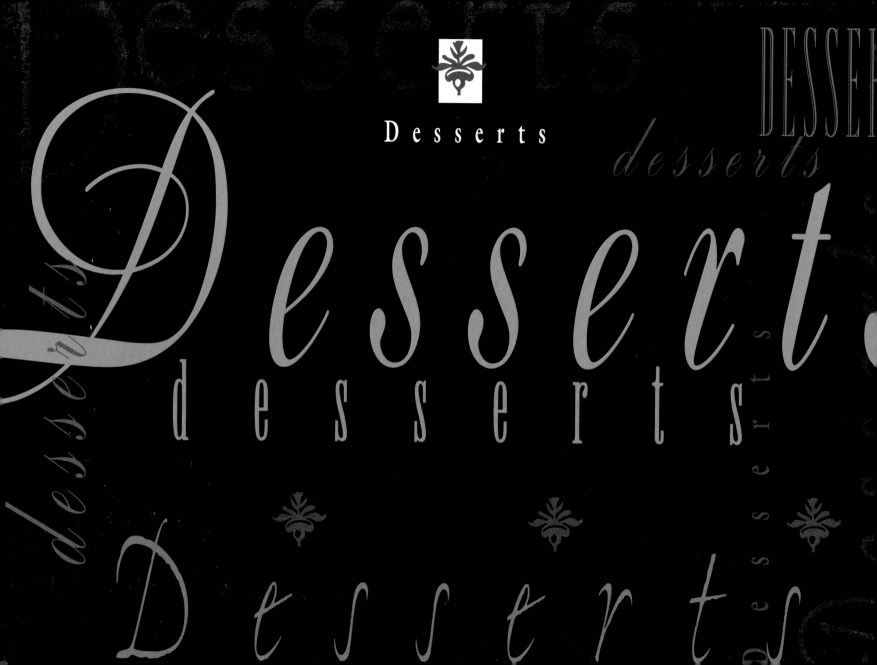

Desserts

Hawaiian Heaven Cake
119

Pineapple Upside Down Cake
122

Peach Surprise Pie
121

Hawaiian Pumpkin Pie
124

Luau Bread
121

Hawaiian Trifle
125

Desserts

HAWAIIAN HEAVEN CAKE

serves ten to twelve

Cake:

3/4 cup sugar
1/4 cup shortening
2 eggs
1 cup *Yoshida's®Hawaiian Sweet & Sour Sauce*
2 cups flour
2 1/2 teaspoons baking powder
1/2 teaspoon salt

1/2 teaspoon nutmeg
1/4 teaspoon cloves
1/2 cup pineapple tidbits, drained
1/2 cup diced fresh peaches
1/2 cup diced fresh oranges
1/2 cup diced fresh apples

Topping:

1/2 cup sugar
1/2 teaspoon cinnamon
1/4 cup melted butter
1/4 cup *Yoshida's®Hawaiian Sweet & Sour Sauce*
1 1/2 cups flour

❧ In a large bowl, beat sugar, shortening and eggs until light. Stir in *Yoshida's®* and blend.

❧ In a small bowl, sift the flour, baking powder, salt, nutmeg and cloves. Add flour mixture to the egg mixture slowly and gently blend. Fold in diced fruit, do not overmix. Spread batter into a 9"x13" baking pan. Set aside.

❧ Make topping by combining sugar, cinnamon, melted butter and *Yoshida's®.* Add flour gradually until mixture is crumbly. Sprinkle topping evenly over batter.

❧ Bake cake on middle rack of oven for 45–60 minutes, or until toothpick comes out clean when inserted into middle of the cake.

❧ Remove cake from oven and let cool for 30 minutes before slicing. Serve warm or cold with whipped cream.

Alice Volkens   Jackson, NJ

Hawaiian Heaven Cake

Peach Surprise Pie

serves six to eight

2   8 ounce packages Neufchatel cheese, softened
1/4 cup sugar
1/2 teaspoon vanilla
1/4 cup *Yoshida's® Hawaiian Sweet & Sour Sauce*
1 prebaked 9" pie crust
1   16 ounce can peach slices, drained
1/4 cup red raspberry preserves
1 teaspoon lemon juice
fresh mint leaves *(optional)*

❧   In the bowl of an electric mixer, blend the Neufchatel cheese, sugar, vanilla and *Yoshida's.®*

❧   Spread the mixture over the bottom of the prepared crust and chill a few hours or overnight.

❧   Just before serving, arrange peach slices decoratively on filling. Mix the preserves with the lemon juice and spoon in between the peach slices.

❧   Garnish with fresh mint.

Luau Bread

serves twenty

4 eggs
2 cups sugar
1/2 cup oil
1 teaspoon vanilla
1 cup diced pineapple
1 cup *Yoshida's® Hawaiian Sweet & Sour Sauce*
1 cup chopped macadamia nuts
2 cups grated zucchini, drained

4 cups flour
1 1/2 teaspoons baking powder
1 1/2 teaspoons baking soda
1 teaspoon salt
1 teaspoon cinnamon
1 cup shredded coconut
1 fresh pineapple, sliced

❧   Preheat oven to 350° F. Grease and flour two loaf pans. Set aside.

❧   In a large bowl, beat eggs until smooth, add sugar and blend. Add oil, vanilla, pineapple, *Yoshida's,®* nuts and zucchini. Blend gently.

❧   In another bowl, mix together flour, baking powder, baking soda, salt, cinnamon and 1/4 cup coconut. Add into the wet ingredients and stir gently. Divide evenly into prepared pans, bake in middle of oven for 45–60 minutes, or until a toothpick inserted into the middle comes out clean. Let cool on a rack for a half hour.

❧   Unmold cakes onto a platter, slice and serve with remaining coconut and pineapple slices.

Desserts

Alice Volkens   Jackson, NJ

PINEAPPLE UPSIDE DOWN CAKE

serves ten to twelve

6 tablespoons unsalted butter

1/2 cup packed dark brown sugar

3 tablespoons dark rum

1 20 ounce can pineapple slices, drained *(reserve 3 tablespoons of juice)*

1/4 cup pecan halves

1/2 cup unsalted margarine, room temperature

3/4 cup granulated sugar

2 eggs

1 teaspoon vanilla extract

1/3 cup *Yoshida's®Hawaiian Sweet & Sour Sauce*

2 cups all purpose flour

1 teaspoon ground ginger

1 1/2 teaspoons baking soda

1/2 teaspoon salt

vanilla ice cream or whipped cream *(optional)*

❧ Preheat oven to 350° F.

❧ Melt the butter and pour into a 9 1/2" springform pan. Wrap the outside of the pan with aluminum foil and place on a baking sheet. Press brown sugar evenly over the bottom of pan and sprinkle with 2 tablespoons of rum. Arrange 7 pineapple slices over the sugar and fill in spaces with pecan halves. Set aside.

❧ In a bowl of a mixer, cream together margarine and sugar. Beat in the eggs, one at a time. Beat in vanilla.

❧ Puree remaining 3 pineapple slices with remaining 1 tablespoon rum and *Yoshida's®* in a blender or food processor. Beat into the butter mixture.

❧ Sift together the flour, ginger, baking soda and salt and beat into the butter mixture alternately with the reserved pineapple juice.

❧ Pour the batter over the pineapple slices in the springform pan. Bake 30–35 minutes or until golden brown and center springs back when gently touched. While cake is still hot, remove the sides of the pan and invert onto a serving plate.

❧ *Serve with ice cream or whipped cream if desired.*

Hawaiian Pumpkin Pie

Hawaiian Pumpkin Pie

makes one nine-inch pie

1 unbaked 9" deep dish pie shell
2 eggs
1 16 ounce can solid pack pumpkin
1/2 cup granulated sugar
1 teaspoon cinnamon
2 teaspoons pumpkin pie spice
1/8 teaspoon ground cloves
1/2 cup *Yoshida's® Hawaiian Sweet & Sour Sauce*
1/4 cup diced raisins or figs *(optional)*
1 12 ounce can evaporated milk
whipped cream *(optional)*

❧ Preheat oven to 425° F. Place pie shell on a baking sheet.

❧ In a large mixing bowl, lightly beat the eggs. Add remaining ingredients, in order given and pour into the pie shell.

❧ Place pie on the middle rack of the oven and bake for 15 minutes. Reduce temperature to 350° F. and continue baking for 45–55 minutes or until center of pie is set. (A knife inserted near the center should come out clean.)

❧ Let pie cool 15 minutes before slicing. Serve with freshly whipped cream if desired.

Alice Volkens   Jackson, NJ

Desserts

HAWAIIAN TRIFLE

serves ten to twelve

2 3 1/8 ounce packages vanilla pudding pie filling mix
2 cups milk
1 1/4 cup chilled pineapple juice
2 cups whipping cream
1/4 cup *Yoshida's® Hawaiian Sweet & Sour Sauce*

1 16 ounce package frozen pound cake, thawed
1/2 cup cream sherry
1 cup heated raspberry jam
1 20 ounce can crushed pineapple
Maraschino cherries (*optional*)

❧ Prepare pudding mix according to package directions, using the milk and pineapple juice listed above to replace the liquid called for in the directions. Cool pudding by putting the saucepan in a larger bowl filled with ice water, stirring often. When cool, transfer to a medium–sized mixing bowl.

❧ In a small bowl, whip 1 cup cream until soft peaks form. Fold the cream into pudding. Stir in *Yoshida's®* and set aside in the refrigerator.

❧ Cut pound cake in half lengthwise and pour the sherry over cake. Cut the cake into 2" pieces. Set aside.

❧ In a 3–quart glass serving bowl spoon in 1 cup of the pudding and spread over bottom of dish. Top with half of the cake pieces, then with half of the raspberry jam. Put 1/2 of the pineapple into a small bowl and reserve for garnish. Put 1/2 of the remaining pineapple on top of the jam in the serving bowl. Spoon half of the remaining pudding on top of the pineapple, then repeat layering process with remaining ingredients, ending with pudding. Refrigerate, covered overnight.

❧ In the bowl of an electric mixer, beat remaining 1 cup cream until soft peaks form, then spread over trifle. Drain reserved pineapple and use it to garnish trifle. Top with Maraschino cherries if desired.

NOTES

INDEX